Anxiety:
Practical About Panic

A practical guide to understanding and
overcoming anxiety disorder

Joshua Fletcher

JOHN
MURRAY
LEARNING

First published in Great Britain in 2019 by John Murray Learning, an imprint of John Murray Press, a division of Hodder and Stoughton Ltd. An Hachette UK company.

British Library Cataloguing in Publication Data: a catalogue record for this title is available from the British Library.

ISBN 978 1 529 32517 1

eBook ISBN 978 1 529 32518 8

Typeset by Cenveo® Publisher Services.

Printed and bound in Great Britain by Clays Ltd, Elcograf S.p.A.

Hachette UK policy is to use papers that are natural, renewable and recyclable products and made from wood grown in sustainable forests. The logging and manufacturing processes are expected to conform to the environmental regulations of the country of origin.

Carmelite House
50 Victoria Embankment
London EC4Y 0DZ
www.hodder.co.uk

I dedicate this book to all my clients, readers of my previous book and to those who are struggling with anxiety. This book is also dedicated to my late brother Harry, my loving and supportive Mum, my late Dad and my wonderful partner Hannah.

The illustrations in this book were created by talented artist Bella Dane, who can be contacted at:

belladanedesign@gmail.com

Contents

PART 4

PART 5

Introduction

It has been a remarkable four years since the release of my first book, *Anxiety: Panicking about Panic*. Since then, I have left the teaching profession and focused solely on developing my knowledge of the various facets of anxiety. This has included studying to become a fully qualified psychotherapist, as well as completing an MSc in Counselling Psychology at Keele University. In May 2015 I set up my own private counselling and coaching practice called The Panic Room, which has been overwhelmingly successful. The experiences and knowledge I have gained through working full-time in the profession have been hugely influential in the creation of this book.

That said, I have endeavoured to convey the information in this book in a similar fashion to my previous one; what you will find is a very personable and user-friendly approach with no confusing academic jargon. As someone who has lived with anxiety for many years, I can understand how overwhelming life can already be, never mind attempting to read an exhaustive text that would often best be used as a doorstop.

This is why the introduction will be left just here. I invite you to engage the best you can with what I have provided in this book and I wish you well in what I believe to be a very achievable recovery.

The Symptoms of an Anxiety or Panic Problem

Psychological Symptoms

Excessive worry

Panic attacks

Derealisation (feeling lucid and detached from surroundings)

Depersonalisation (feeling detached from persona/personality)

Feeling apprehensive

Hypochondria (the fear that you're seriously ill)

The fear of a panic attack

Body checking (looking for signs of illness)

Repetitive and looping thoughts

Feeling terrified

Obsessive thoughts

Inability to relax

Difficulty completing tasks

Feeling hopeless and depressed

Overactive imagination

Agoraphobia (fear of going outside)

Fear of other people's opinions

Fear of embarrassment

Fear that you're developing a psychological illness

Self-analysing (similar to body checking, above)

Negative thoughts of isolation

Deep level of focus about personal 'identity'

Loss of appetite

Big increase in appetite

Loss of libido

Loss of interest in work

Loss of interest in doing things that were once enjoyable

Depressive thoughts

Dwelling on thoughts

Constantly trying to work out how to feel 'normal' again

Constantly feeling tired

Dampened sense of humour

Inability to focus

Physical Symptoms

Heart palpitations (short bursts of a rapid heartbeat)

Headaches – constant or recurring

Light-headedness

Exhaustion

Constant lethargy

Irregular bowel movements

Chest pains (ache)

Chest pains (sharp stabbing)

Bloating

Tickling/fluttering sensation in chest and oesophagus

Nausea

Constant pacing

Dizziness

Perspiration (sweating frequently)

Tinnitus (ringing ears)

Stomach cramps

Eye floaters (particle-like objects that 'float' in front of vision)

Symptoms of Irritable Bowel Syndrome (IBS)

Rib pain

Rib discomfort (feeling pressure under ribs)

Stomach grumbling

Dry mouth

Feeling tired after eating

Abdominal pains

Shooting pains in back and abdomen

Neck ache and pains

Ache behind eyes

Erectile dysfunction

Jaw ache and tenderness

PART 1

You're in Good Company

Hello, my name is Josh. A sincere thank you for purchasing this book. I'm a fully qualified psychotherapist who specialises in working with people with anxiety disorders – something that I've been doing with a high degree of success for the past five years. I have also previously been diagnosed with an anxiety disorder and have lived through years of crippling fear, wrestling with a constant sense of dread and continually avoiding things because of that fear. I'm not talking about your usual fear; I mean the kind of fear that seemingly comes from nowhere and leaves you questioning your own sanity, where you're afraid to do the things that you once used to do for fear of losing a sense of control. I recall spending endless days fending off panic attacks and chasing my own breath, as well as trying to 'figure out' why I felt the way I did. That said, I'm okay now! These days I enjoy spending my time helping others with anxiety, whilst living a normal life free from the clutches of thought-consuming fear.

I have written this book from the perspective of someone who has experienced anxiety first-hand, and have drawn upon my academic studies as well as my knowledge as a practising psychotherapist. There are many books about anxiety out there, but I hope the personable approach of this book will help you feel at ease reading about a sensitive subject.

To get us started, I'm going to list some of the most common beliefs about anxiety that both my clients and I have shared in the past. If you can relate to any of them, then this book should be able to help you.

'Something isn't quite right with me.'

If you have noticed that you don't quite feel like your usual, calm self, then this could be the first sign of an anxiety problem. I can relate to many of my clients when they state that they just don't feel like they used to, where their main attention is focused on a sense of fear and unease rather than continuing with normal day-to-day routines and behaviours. You may feel like you're constantly on edge, or frantically trying to distract yourself from experiencing the full force of how you feel. It is very common for people to have their days dictated by a feeling of apprehension and excessive worry, which perhaps contrasts to how they usually, or used to, function. Perhaps you often compare how you are now to a time where these feelings of unease didn't seem to take precedence. Maybe you wonder why this has happened, since it hasn't really troubled you before. Fear not, as this is okay; it doesn't mean anything dangerous is about to happen. It is incredibly likely to be an anxiety problem.

'I'm scared for no reason. Why on earth do I feel scared?'

My problems with anxiety began when I noticed that I started to feel scared for little to no reason. This is often pinpointed as the start of an anxiety problem, or anxiety disorder, by many of my clients. Sometimes I thought there *was* a reason, like blaming people, crowded spaces, tiredness, work, relationships, diet, you name it. However, in hindsight, I realised that these were just excuses to pin to the fact that I was disproportionately scared in any situation that I found myself in. On top of this, I also felt a bit 'spacey' and weird – something called derealisation. I thought that I was the only person who had experienced this. Now, if you give an analytical brain like mine problems such as fear for no reason and feeling weird, then you could assume that I would try to naturally work this problem out.

Unfortunately for me, I found the process of 'working this out' to be counter-productive: the process of trying to find a solution only added to the fear, as I could never really find an answer to the problem. If you fast-forward eight years, you'll now find me in my anxiety practice working with people with a similar mindset. If you find that your days are often filled with unknown fear, and you may be feeling a bit spacey and detached from your surroundings, then fear not, as you're in good company. There's nothing dangerous about this feeling and you can return to a sense of calm in due course.

Fear of losing your mind

I can't tell you how many times I have worked with people who feel like they're losing their mind. I, too, at one point, used to spend sunrise to sunset ruminating on whether the intense feeling of dread I was feeling was there because I'd finally 'lost it'. Rest assured that anxiety, namely the anxious response, cannot make you lose your mind. However, the anxious response can feel scary and it does like to think it can trick you into thinking you can lose control. Just remember, it doesn't matter how many times you have panicked, the anxious response is not hurting your brain, nor causing it any permanent damage. You are not losing control. If this is applicable to you, then rest assured, you are in good company.

Panic attacks, then fearing they'll happen again

A panic attack can be described as an intense feeling of fear and dread that's usually perpetuated by a lack of attributable cause. Panic attacks can severely scare people to the extent that they fear them happening again – ultimately a fear of fear itself. Further to this, fearing panic attacks ties in with the same fears around 'losing our minds', where the theme of control, or losing control, plays an important part in keeping the fear there. I remember a time where I avoided everything 'just in case' I had a panic attack. This applied to leaving the house, seeing friends, going to work, or even going to the supermarket. I used to pace the house trying to work out why on earth I was panicking all the time, whilst at the same time avoiding doing normal things, just in case they caused me to lose control and have another panic attack. This behaviour is very common, so don't think you are alone if this resonates with you.

If you feel panicky when reading this book, or at any other time, there's an *Emergency Panic Attack Help* section at the end of this book that you can use as an aid to ground yourself. It's a transcript that I used to use at the height of my problems with anxiety and a tool that my clients and readers of my previous book report to be very helpful.

Avoiding things

It is not only the fear of panic that can persuade someone to avoid doing things. Sometimes people who feel slightly anxious may feel they lack the confidence to partake in activities that they once deemed normal. This can include going to work, socialising, visiting family or just simply leaving the house. If you have noticed that you have been avoiding doing things of late, then rest assured that this is okay and that you can build or reclaim that confidence.

Weird bodily changes

What I have mentioned so far all relates to the *feelings* associated with having an anxiety problem. However, anxiety can come with an abundance of physical symptoms too, some of which are listed at the start of this book. I recall fixating on heart palpitations, chest pains, my digestive cycle, muscle twitching and spasms, strange floating things in my vision, a sore jaw, tinnitus, headaches – just to name a few. There is a seemingly endless list of physical symptoms associated with prolonged anxiety and stress. I spend a lot of time with new clients assuring them that, if the doctor says the symptoms are nothing dangerous, then we can conclude that they're just part of an anxiety problem.

Reassurance

A large proportion of my clients have disclosed that they have spent a lot of time seeking different forms of reassurance in order to help them understand why they feel the way they do. I recall spending days trawling search engines for explanations and signs of hope that I could change the way I felt. Some of my clients disclosed that a lot of their personal relationships were strained because they relied on close members of family to constantly reassure them that they were okay. If you have been struggling to reassure yourself that you're okay, then this book will help. I believe that education about anxiety goes such a long way towards understanding it and reclaiming some control.

The aim of this book

Please rest assured that you're in good company when reading this book. Sometimes we avoid reading anxiety-related topics for fear of triggering the anxious response. If this happens during reading, then this is completely okay. Nothing bad will result from it and it will only serve to further your understanding of it. I have written this book to help you as much as I can – drawing upon my own personal experiences and those of working with hundreds of people as a psychotherapist who specialises in anxiety disorders. I've organised the book in a way that structures my approach as a step-by-step system.

As I don't know you personally, I invite you to meet me halfway and apply the parts of the book that relate to you and your situation. I sincerely hope that you enjoy and gain something from this book and from any future publications that I release. I will endeavour to keep normalising the topic of anxiety for people like you and share everything that I learn on the way.

What is Anxiety?

Anxiety as a feeling

The feeling of anxiety is something that you're perhaps experiencing right now as you hold this book. This skilful use of deductive reasoning comes from assuming that you're not reading this book in order to improve your baking skills, but doing so in order to try and read up on a subject that has afflicted your life for some time now.

I sincerely hope that this book, along with my previous one, goes some way towards helping you in your understanding of anxiety and your goal of overcoming the condition. If you haven't yet read *Anxiety: Panicking about Panic*, then I strongly recommend that you do so, as it will help you get the most out of this book. That said, this is not mandatory.

Anxiety is usually characterised by feelings of unease, dread and fearful anticipation. Perhaps you're finding it difficult in the present moment to concentrate, sit still and ignore the negative thoughts and feelings that come with feeling anxious. A large proportion of my clients (as well as myself at one point) have, at one time, complained of living the majority of each day with a general sense of unease, whilst at the same time listening and observing the anxious mind as it toys with the imagination – our days often crammed full of catastrophic thoughts, 'What if?' scenarios and a general worry that we've 'gone bananas'.

Much like feelings of hunger or tiredness, anxiety is a 'normal' psychological response that everybody feels at some point. However, anxiety can become a problem when we deem it to be *excessive*, or perhaps not appropriate given the context. Some examples of common, excessive anxiety are:

- **Catastrophising**, e.g. fear of serious illness, death, losing a loved one, or imagining the worst-case scenario in a given situation
- **Panic attacks**, e.g. loss of control, fear of going insane
- **Feeling like we're about to break**, e.g. when leaving the house, pushing our energy levels too far
- **Obsessive thoughts**, e.g. constant worrying, looping thoughts, inability to change focus
- **Generalised anxiety**, e.g. can't sit still, need to feel productive, must have something to worry about

With excessive anxiety, it is ever so common to be stuck questioning why we feel the way we do, or trying to ascribe fatalistic reasons that match the feeling of being anxious and frightened. For the average person, it's usually easy to ascribe a reason for any current feeling but, for the excessively anxious person, the cause isn't always identifiable, which often makes us panic further about why we feel the way we do. We are often resigned to assuming that the *worst-case scenario* of our current situation is inevitable.

EVERYTHING
AROUND ME IS FINE

BUT I ANTICIPATED
THE WORST

If you refer to the 'Symptoms of Anxiety' section at the beginning of this book, you will see a list of physical and psychological symptoms that have all been linked to anxiety. This links in to the idea of anxiety 'as a feeling', due to the condition leading to an overabundance of physical ailments such as back pain, migraines, headaches, neck pain, shoulder pain, stomach and bowel pain.

Furthermore, and perhaps most poignantly, the phenomenon of panic attacks seems to epitomise excessive anxiety. A panic attack occurs when the only reasoning we can apportion to a feeling of fear is the imminent loss of control. This then 'snowballs' the feeling of anxiety, as the prospect of losing control is frightening to many people. There's a comprehensive overview of panic attacks in my previous book, *Anxiety: Panicking about Panic*, so please feel free to switch for reference. I will also be referring to them several times throughout this book but within a fresh new context.

There are several medical conditions (or anxiety disorders) that revolve around the feeling of excessive anxiety. These include:

- **Agoraphobia** – Excessive worry about the outside
- **Health Anxiety** – Excessive worry about health and symptoms
- **Anxiety and Panic Disorder** – Excessive worry about panic
- **Social Anxiety** – Excessive fear of the judgement of others and how we are perceived

If you're reading this and thinking 'I can relate to this', then please rest assured that you're not going insane. Anxiety is incredibly common and can be overcome with understanding and a bit of work. It's common to feel hopeless at times, but

I've seen enough positive work with anxiety to believe that anyone can overcome the condition.

Do I have an anxiety problem?

So far, we have established that anxiety can be divided into 'normal' and 'excessive' levels, so how do we know if excessive anxiety has become a problem? For this section, I have used an extract from my previous book, *Anxiety: Panicking about Panic.*

The first step to identifying excessive anxiety is when we realise that something isn't quite right with our mind and body. Perhaps you don't feel the way you 'used to', or feel that your days are often dictated by odd feelings of apprehension and worry. It's also likely that you've often found yourself being struck with bouts of unexplainable panic, which can often trigger a chain of events where you may ultimately begin to panic about the state of panicking itself.

On top of anxious thoughts or even panic attacks, maybe you're experiencing feelings of constant worry, states of derealisation (detachment from self and surroundings), an inability to relax, strange bodily changes and symptoms of depression. Believe it or not, these are all common symptoms of an anxiety condition. Anxiety actually has an overabundance of symptoms, some of which you may have stumbled across at the start of this book. These symptoms, which range from the obvious to the obscure, are all linked with anxiety in some way.

The classic and most common sign of an anxiety problem is when we find that our days are mostly being dictated by feelings of intense and unexplainable fear, and that we may begin to perceive everything around us as different and somewhat 'detached'. Further to this, panic may have crept into our lives, which can act as a focus point for our worries to be directed towards. This fear can easily lead us to question things such as our health or our perception of reality and to expect the most unlikely of worst-case scenarios.

Below are some of the common assumptions that the standard anxiety sufferer can often relate to:

Anxiety assumptions

- I feel terrified for no logical reason.
- I haven't felt normal for a long time; something must be wrong.
- Why am I scared to do 'normal' things?
- A psychological condition must be the cause of this change.
- I must have a serious health problem, i.e. heart failure, cancer.
- My brain/mind does not work like other people's.
- I don't think this is ever going to go away. I can't handle it.
- No one else fully understands what I'm going through.
- Why do I feel like I'm about to die?

Furthermore, it is important that we look at some of the most common *physical* symptoms that signal an anxiety problem. The symptoms section at the start of this book supplies a comprehensive list of symptoms that have all been linked to anxiety; below are some I have found to be the most common:

Common physical symptoms

- **Heart** – palpitations, chest flutters, 'skipping a beat', heart pounding, hyperawareness of heartbeat
- **Abdominal pains** – chest pains and tightness, stomach pains and cramping
- **Derealisation** – sense of unreality, an illusory detachment from surroundings, shutdown of peripheral vision, difficulty focusing
- **Head** – constant and prolonged headaches, light-headedness, dizziness, vertigo, tinnitus, sensitivity to light, eye floaters
- **Energy** – tiredness, lethargy, 'heavy head', exhaustion
- **Pain** – unfamiliar aches and pains, cramps, rib pain, muscle tension pain, dental pain
- **IBS** – indigestion, constipation, acid reflux, trapped wind, diarrhoea, gut and intestinal pains

If you feel that you can relate to any of the listed anxiety assumptions and to several of the physical symptoms listed here and at the start of this book, then it would be a pretty safe bet to assume that you have an anxiety problem. For more information, or for a sense of reassurance, I suggest that you also read my first book.

The best feedback I receive from readers and clients is that my first book provides immediate reassurance and a sense of relief that immediately addresses what I have explained above. This book has been written as the follow-up to that book, so please forgive me for shifting the focus from reassurance to a more pragmatic approach.

Anxiety as a bodily process

We've looked at anxiety as a *feeling*, but it is vital to understand it from a biological perspective. I feel this goes some way to addressing the confusion surrounding feeling excessively anxious. At my practice, I aim to do this as soon as possible, as it highlights the brain and body duality that's at the core of every anxiety condition.

Fight-or-flight response

It is more than likely that you've heard the phrase 'fight or flight' at some point in your life, whether it's from trawling through books about anxiety, or paying attention during science lessons at school. In my experience, I have found that doctors (the well-informed ones, anyway) will often attempt to explain the *fight-or-flight response* in an attempt to reassure their anxious patients. I will, however, put it within a context that is understandable by drawing from my research and my previous book.

The fight–or–flight (or *acute stress*) response is a genetically inherited, psychological and physiological response to a perceived danger or threat. For example, if a rabid bear came crashing through your window, you'd quickly come to terms with a very high level of the acute stress response. Adrenaline would be released, your muscles would tense up, your thoughts would race, then you'd either fight the bear or run for your life!

Below is an extract from the book *Breakfast of Champions* by one of my favourite authors, Kurt Vonnegut. It breaks down the fight-or-flight response that the character Kilgore experiences whilst being lunged at by a giant, aggressive dog. This comprehensive description takes place over one second:

'My eyes told my mind about him. My mind sent a message to my hypothalamus, told it to release the hormone CRF into the short vessels connecting my hypothalamus and my pituitary gland. The CRF inspired my pituitary gland to dump the hormone ACTH into my bloodstream. My pituitary had been making and storing ACTH for such an occasion…

> ...some of the ACTH in my bloodstream
> reached the outer shell of my adrenal
> gland, which had been making and storing
> glucocorticoids for emergencies. My
> adrenal gland added glucocorticoids to my
> bloodstream. They went all over my body,
> changing glycogen into glucose. Glucose was
> muscle food. It would help me fight like a wildcat
> or run like a deer...'

Perhaps the most important part of the passage lies in the last paragraph, which is as follows:

> '...My adrenal gland gave me a shot of
> *adrenaline*, too. I turned purple as my blood
> pressure skyrocketed. The *adrenaline* made my
> heart go like a burglar alarm. It also stood my hair
> on end. It also caused coagulants to pour into
> my bloodstream so, in case I was wounded, my
> vital juices wouldn't drain away.'

I am conscious that this overview of the fight-or-flight response could be a tad overwhelming, especially if you're feeling anxious right now. You're presumably not reading this book whilst being attacked by a feral animal either. Therefore, I would like us to simplify and concentrate on the most important part of the process that's primarily responsible for making us feel the *fear* and the *thoughts* surrounding anxiety and panic.

This important component is the chemical *adrenaline* – a hormone at the core of almost every anxiety problem.

Adrenaline

Adrenaline, also known as epinephrine, is a hormone that is produced by the adrenal glands, which can be found above each of our kidneys. It is also referred to as the 'fight-or-flight' hormone, which ties in nicely with what I'm about to explain.

If you are feeling anxious, on edge, apprehensive or panicky, then you are also feeling the effects of adrenaline. If you're waking up feeling worried and fearful, then this is also adrenaline. Perhaps you have experienced a panic attack in the past? This, too, is adrenaline.

It is incredibly important to understand the prominent role adrenaline plays when living with anxiety. It is responsible for numerous feelings and thoughts associated with the condition, as well as being linked with a significant number of physical symptoms. Simply put, you know when you've got adrenaline in the bloodstream when you find yourself feeling scared and frozen in a state of negative anticipation.

Adrenaline isn't necessarily a bad chemical, though, as it contributes to feelings of excitement, healthy competition, sexual arousal, having fun and positive anticipation. It can become a problem, however, when it becomes excessive, hence the link between *excessive* anxiety and *excessive* adrenaline.

With regard to anxiety and panic disorder, adrenaline is primarily responsible for:

- **a change in thoughts** – racing thoughts, believing the worst-case scenario, finding the dangers, imagining a catastrophe, over-thinking why we feel the way we do
- **a change in feelings** – feelings of dread, doom, feeling like something awful is about to happen, fear, terror, angst
- **physical symptoms** – heart palpitations, light-headedness, feeling detached, IBS, chest pains, headaches, dizziness (and more listed at the start of this book).

Throughout my research and working with clients at my practice, I've heard a lot of similar complaints from those whose lives are dictated by anxiety and excessive adrenaline. Some of these complaints revolve around the following paraphrases:

- 'I find myself panicking for no reason.'
- 'I don't feel like I used to and I'm worried about it.'
- 'I obsess over physical symptoms like heart palpitations and derealisation.'
- 'I'm scared of having a panic attack!'
- 'I have panic attacks every day.'
- 'I avoid leaving the house due to fearing how I will feel.'
- 'I'm losing hope that I will ever get better.'
- 'I keep replaying that conversation with that person over and over again.'
- 'I just feel like something awful is about to happen.'

If you can relate to these statements, then I once again urge
you to read my previous book, *Anxiety: Panicking about Panic*,
as it addresses these worries and goes some way towards
reassuring you. The book also guides you to an understanding
of where these worries come from and how to address
them. For now, though, I'm going to assume that you're well
associated with adrenaline and its effects on the body, as well
as the feelings and symptoms it can cause.

Panic attacks

A panic attack is when an intense feeling of fear, dread, loss
of control and entrapment overwhelms a person. It's also the
cue from the brain to release large amounts of adrenaline
into the body. To the uninformed, panic attacks usually have
no identifiable trigger and strike seemingly from nowhere.
Accompanying these feelings are thoughts of an imminent
disaster, impending doom and even fear of sudden death.

The number of anxiety sufferers I have spoken to who have ended up in the emergency room with no explainable symptoms borders on the absurd!

A panic attack leads you down roads of irrational thinking, where even the most intelligent people are forced to feel and believe in the most unlikely of outcomes. Personally, I used to whirl up in a panic over a chest flutter, headache, variations in breathing, stomach cramps, detachment from surroundings, etc.

Along with these feelings are other physical symptoms that occur when panic has struck. A panic attack causes our muscles to tense up, our peripheral vision to shut down (tunnel vision) and alters the way we breathe – tricking us into thinking we're not getting enough oxygen. It also causes light-headedness, dizziness and sometimes nausea. Below are the main symptoms and feelings that occur during a panic attack:

- Sudden and intense fright
- A sense of derealisation / detachment from surroundings
- Chest pains
- Pounding or thumping chest
- Fast heart rate
- Difficulty maintaining a steady pace of breathing
- Irrational thinking, i.e. *Am I going to die? Is this a heart attack? I must have a serious condition like cancer.*
- Chest fluttering / heart palpitations
- Racing thoughts and confusion
- The urge to do anything but be stationary, i.e. pace the room or squeeze an object
- Tunnel vision
- An overwhelming urge to 'escape' or run away

A panic attack can occur when the body releases a large amount of unexpected adrenaline into the bloodstream. I mentioned before that adrenaline can cause all sorts of changes both physically and mentally, so if we're unprepared or 'caught off guard' by a newly released dump of adrenaline, then it could be expected that we would panic about this sudden change.

The panic arises from the *confusion* about what is happening, and this works in tandem with a belief that we cannot cope. Adrenaline actually causes our minds to race and be filled with all sorts of thoughts and conclusions as to *why* we're panicking and *why* we're feeling strange.

This would explain why so many people are convinced that they're having a heart attack, or that they're going insane, or that they have an incurable condition, and so on. It is the adrenaline that affects our rationality during these periods of panic, thus causing them to turn into prolonged *panic attacks.*

These panic attacks don't last forever because the adrenal gland finally becomes exhausted and cannot release any further adrenaline. The reader should take comfort from the fact that a panic attack cannot last forever because of this and the feeling of normality will return – at least until the adrenal gland has recharged and we may unknowingly fall back into the same repetitive thought habit.

Anxiety: two simplified biological components

There are two components of anxiety that need to be focused on to develop a thorough understanding of it. The first component is what we have covered so far – the wonderful chemical, adrenaline. Many people can come to terms with the concept of having to deal with excessive adrenaline, but it inevitably leaves questions revolving around the concept of where the excess adrenaline has come from.

'Ok, so I acknowledge I've got loads of adrenaline flowing through my veins every time I'm feeling anxious, but where has this come from? And how do I stop it?'

This leads to the second most important contributor to feeling excessively anxious: the function of the body's *nervous system*. In a nutshell, when the body's nervous system is overstimulated, the body releases disproportionate amounts of adrenaline.

It is imperative that we learn and understand the role of the nervous system in relation to anxiety. Once we have grasped how both adrenaline and the nervous system operate, we can begin to explore how we can make ourselves feel better. This is something that I and many others have done since learning about anxiety and, perhaps most importantly, it starts off a process of learning about ourselves.

The nervous system

The body's nervous system can be separated into two parts. These are:

1 The Voluntary System

2 The Autonomic System.

The Voluntary System is mostly concerned with movement and feeling sensations. It involves lots of motor and sensory nerves to help us move, touch and feel. For example, if you lift your arm over your head to change a light bulb, the brain sends signals to activate the voluntary nervous system, which in turn triggers motor and sensory nerves in order to move our arm and feel the light bulb within our grasp. The Voluntary System, however, is of no concern to us when trying to understand and overcome excessive anxiety.

The Autonomic System is where I would like us to bring our attention. It is both the *cause* and the *solution* to easing anxiety and the symptoms that come with it. The Autonomic Nervous System has two branches. These are:

1 The Sympathetic Nervous System

2 The Parasympathetic Nervous System

THE SYMPATHETIC SYSTEM

The ironically named 'sympathetic' system is responsible for triggering the body's fight-or-flight response. It is responsible for stimulating nerves that activate the adrenal glands, as well as altering the function of vital organs when faced with 'danger'. Nerves, accompanied by adrenaline, send blood to the brain and to our muscles which, in turn, increases our heart rate and blood pressure. Furthermore, and perhaps most importantly, it also causes the mind to race in order to identify any danger that we may be facing.

When we're in fight-or-flight mode, the sympathetic nervous system – through the use of the adrenal glands and the thyroid – causes a huge release of energy to help us either fight or run away from a perceived danger. This is when we feel the fear that almost defines anxiety.

'This is all well and good, Josh. I understand.
But why am I feeling this at home, or at work,
when there is no danger? I simply don't need to
have this response in my life.'

Excessive anxiety occurs when the sympathetic nervous system becomes overstimulated. As mentioned before, and I will highlight this again because of its importance, *an overstimulated nervous system causes the body to release disproportionate amounts of adrenaline.*

If you're panicking about physical symptoms, your mental well-being, the way you feel, social anxiety, the outside world or health anxiety, then you're *exploring the thoughts caused by an overstimulated sympathetic nervous system.* Hence why people catastrophise, have panic attacks or live each day in a state of fear. Thoughts that once meant nothing to us suddenly become really important!

It is the excess adrenaline, caused by the overstimulated nervous system, that forces us to contend with reacting to frightening thoughts. When we learn to calm the sympathetic nervous system, then we regulate the adrenal response and become somewhat 'normal' again.

We can view our sympathetic nervous system like a bottle of fizzy pop. If we constantly shake the bottle, without allowing it to rest, then the pressure build-up causes the bottle to burst at the slightest twist of the lid:

ADRENALINE

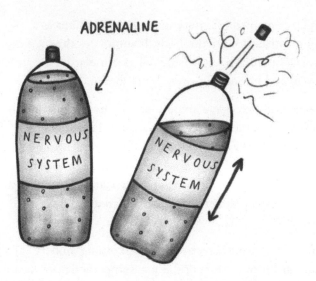

If you have ever had a panic attack, then you will know how exhausting it is to function after you have experienced one. This is because, as well as adrenaline, the sympathetic nervous system has depleted heaps of energy. The body drops its normal day-to-day priorities to deal with all the adrenaline (and cortisol) that the body has released. This is all due to an overstimulated sympathetic nervous system.

You needn't worry though, because I've written this book to teach you how to calm this response and help you on your way to living a normal life again.

THE PARASYMPATHETIC NERVOUS SYSTEM

The other part of our autonomic system is the Parasympathetic Nervous System. This part is activated when we nurture ourselves through relaxation, positive thoughts, self-reassurance and living a balanced life.

The parasympathetic nervous system functions as a regenerative tool for the body. It stimulates the vital organs associated with digestion, as well as stimulating the immune system and promoting overall well-being.

People with excessive anxiety usually live with a significant imbalance in the way their nervous system operates; the sympathetic system operates far more than the parasympathetic. This would go some way to explaining why many people with anxiety often suffer from digestion problems, sleep deficiencies and a scarcity of positive thoughts.

One of the main objectives in overcoming anxiety is to get into a habit of nurturing the parasympathetic nervous system. This part of the nervous system can often get left behind, particularly if anxiety has been present within our lives for a long time.

Summary and Step One

In order to begin being practical about panic, we must firstly understand what anxiety is – both as a feeling and in terms of its biological components. Just remember, at the core of feeling anxious is the chemical adrenaline, which is responsible for both the anxious feelings and the negative, dictating thoughts. If you're feeling anxious right now, it is due to having excess adrenaline on board.

Just remember that having anxiety is OK! Having lots of adrenaline on board is absolutely fine, despite it leading to lots of uncomfortable feelings and sensations. I'm fortunate enough to have spoken to thousands who have overcome the condition of anxiety and nothing 'bad' has happened to them as a result of living with anxiety.

Secondly, we must acknowledge the role of the overstimulated nervous system. The more stimulated our *sympathetic* nervous system, then the more adrenaline the body releases into the bloodstream.

It is important not to overcomplicate our anxiety condition. Having been through an anxiety disorder myself, as well as being a counsellor, I have seen how tempting it is to try to work things out by yourself. However, this ends up being done through the lens of adrenaline. We can hit dead ends, go round in loops and, ultimately, end up back where we started.

For now, let's just remember that it is excess adrenaline and the nervous system at play here. It is responsible for our racing thoughts, our feelings of fear, panic attacks and just generally not feeling ourselves. By aiming to activate our parasympathetic nervous system, through rest, self-reassurance and positive stimulation, we can begin to calm our sympathetic nervous system, which is responsible for the negative feelings associated with anxiety.

With this in mind, let us move on.

PART 2

Putting Anxiety into Perspective

Common habits of the anxious

Changing our perspective on anxiety is an incredibly important element in overcoming any anxiety-related condition. It also goes some way to providing us with a sense of clarity with regard to the ongoing duality between the brain and the body when we find ourselves anxious.

I will begin this part of the book by highlighting some of the most common negative habits, or 'pitfalls', that the anxious person often falls into. By doing this, we can begin to learn the skill of observing our thoughts, as well as learning how to reassure ourselves.

The miracle thought

Have you ever spent hours on end trying to 'work out' why you feel the way you do? Perhaps at many points you have lost patience with feeling anxious and therefore want to find its origins in order to fix it? One common habit when living with anxiety is the urge to try and find the 'miracle thought' that, once discovered, will make all our feelings go away.

At The Panic Room, I often see new clients who have attempted to do their homework before coming to visit me. By 'homework', I mean attempting to construct a form of reasoning for why they feel the way that they do. This reasoning is usually unspecific and often comes from a rhetoric of blame rather than logic. Basically, in an attempt to rationalise our feelings, we try to work everything out.

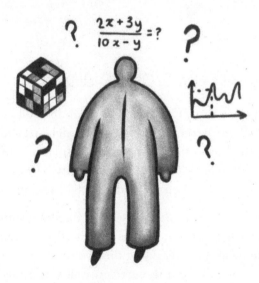

Unfortunately, this approach is the first mistake when trying to ease the feelings of anxiety. Analysing and over-thinking our negative feelings – particularly feelings that worry us – only serves to enhance their importance. In other words, worrying about worry only causes more worry!

What we need is a little patience when we're feeling anxious. The only 'mistake' we have made here is to try to solve our anxiety problem through the eyes of stone-cold logic and assisted by adrenaline. As you'll already be aware, trying to think with adrenaline in our bloodstream can be quite a difficult process. The fight-or-flight response isn't interested in deep, psychological issues; it wants to resolve the problem immediately. This is why a lot of people seem to panic when they cannot find a solution to their problem.

If you've found yourself ruminating through the deep chasms of your mind for the miracle thought that dissolves anxiety, then I advise you to just stop. Remind yourself that this is the work of adrenaline, then channel all of your energy into shifting the focus of your attention to the problem at hand. Rather than giving the anxiety/ adrenaline attention and enhancing its importance, let's work on reassuring ourselves and bringing our anxiety levels down.

Catastrophising

Anxiety often causes us to master the art of catastrophising. Catastrophising occurs when we seem to believe in the worst-case scenario of a given situation. You know you're about to catastrophise when you begin to preface a thought with the phrase *'What if …?'*

Almost every scenario has a spectrum of probability, which is usually regulated by our rational mind. This regulation is also helped when we're producing less adrenaline and our sympathetic nervous system is not overstimulated. When our anxiety levels are high, however, the spectrum of probability in a given scenario becomes skewed, thus leading to irrational assumptions and believing in worst-case scenarios. Let's take a look at these examples:

Scenario:	I can't find my wallet.
Catastrophe:	What if it has been stolen?
Scenario:	I've had a headache for three days.
Catastrophe:	What if I've got a brain tumor?
Scenario:	My friend hasn't called me.
Catastrophe:	What if she secretly hates me?
Scenario:	I need to go to the supermarket.
Catastrophe:	What if I have a panic attack?
Scenario:	I've not felt myself for a while now.
Catastrophe:	What if I'm going insane?
Scenario:	The doctor tried to call me.
Catastrophe:	What if he's found something seriously wrong with me?
Scenario:	I need to do this normal thing that I used to do.
Catastrophe:	What if I lose control?

These are all common examples of catastrophising (the list is endless). It is incredibly important to observe when you are catastrophising and to then use this observation constructively.

I, along with many of my clients, find it helpful to gauge the amount of adrenaline on board by roughly measuring the level of our catastrophising. Basically, the more we believe our irrational thoughts, then the more adrenaline we have to deal with. This is discussed in depth in the section entitled 'The Anxiety Scale'.

Let's look at the spectrum of probability that I mentioned before within the context of a scenario:

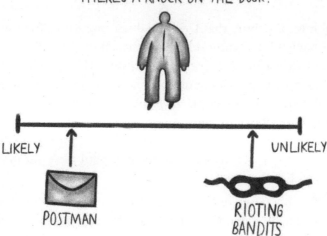

THERE'S A KNOCK ON THE DOOR!

LIKELY   UNLIKELY

POSTMAN   RIOTING BANDITS

By visualizing our thoughts on a spectrum of probability, we can begin to form a rational picture of what is going on. We can begin to challenge the '*What if?*'s and take a step back from automatically believing in the worst outcome of a situation.

Health anxiety, also known as hypochondria, often epitomises catastrophising thoughts and behaviours. For example, a headache is often misinterpreted as a brain tumour, a heart palpitation suddenly becomes a heart problem and indigestion is swiftly deemed evidence of cancer. The excessive anxiety creates a lens that we use to perceive what is happening, rather than engaging the rational side of the brain that sides with probability.

If you've ever had a panic attack, or suffer from them frequently, then you'll be able to relate to feeling like you're constantly at one end of the spectrum. The scary, catastrophic thoughts, accompanied by loads of adrenaline, can be very persuasive in making us believe the worst-case scenario within the current environment. This leads me on nicely to explaining the next common habit.

Avoidance

Habit is something that I will be discussing a lot throughout this book. One common habit of the anxious is feeling the need to *avoid*, or *escape*, certain situations. This is usually characterised by refusing to go to a certain place, avoiding speaking to certain people, or *planning around* something that we might feel may trigger our anxiety. For example:

- 'I want to visit my aunty in the city, but I can't just in case I feel anxious.'
- 'I'm not going to go to work, because the only way I'm keeping my mind together is by staying inside my house.'
- 'I want to visit my friend, but I will walk in the rain rather than use the bus. Buses may trigger my anxiety.'
- 'I need to go grocery shopping, but I'm afraid I will embarrass myself and lose control.'

Supermarkets, for some odd reason, seem to be a common place of avoidance for many people suffering with anxiety. Over time I have worked out the reasoning for this and I challenge you to interpret *why* as you read this book.

It is important to realise that, as anxiety sufferers, we avoid situations for three main reasons:

1 We don't like the feeling of being anxious. We believe and feel like we may lose control.

2 We partly or fully believe in the worst-case scenario of that situation (catastrophising).

3 A combination of the above two points.

It is for these reasons that we avoid doing things that we used to do. A lot of my clients – similar to my own experience –

have highlighted in the initial sessions that they can no longer do things that were once easy for them. The need to avoid seems to outweigh the notion of 'just doing it', because we now believe that we may not cope in these scenarios. This is called a *core belief*, which I will discuss in depth later on. A *negative association* has also been formed with the avoided activities. Associations are something I also discuss later on.

Try to recognise that avoidance is a symptom of anxiety. If you're avoiding doing something – particularly if that something used to be 'normal' for you – then you're seeing the scenario through the eyes of adrenaline. Feeling like you'll lose control, or you'll embarrass yourself, or something 'bad' might happen, is simply the fight-or-flight response trying to convince you that there is a danger in these scenarios. Fear not as we can challenge this in easy, manageable steps.

Escapism

There are two forms of escapism: literal and sensual.

Literal escapism, or 'the need to escape', is very similar to avoidance. It is usually characterised by the need to plan around the anxiety through the use of planned 'escape routes' from a potential 'disaster'. Some examples that I've heard from clients include:

- 'In the cinema I always sit near the entrance. This allows me to easily run outside just in case I start to feel anxious.'
- 'I choose to take the bus rather than the underground train, because I can escape if I'm anxious.'
- 'If I go to this place, then I need to have somebody with me, just in case something bad happens.'

- 'I'll take the stairs rather than the lift, just in case the lift stops and I become anxious.'
- 'I'm going to the concert, but I will stay at the back and memorise the fire exits, just in case something bad happens, or I become anxious.'

With regard to agoraphobia (fear of leaving or straying too far from home), here are some similar statements that are also, quite ironically, forms of escapism:

- 'If I go too far away from my house, I can't escape back to my safe zone.'
- 'I can't go on holiday because I can't escape back to my house.'

Using all these statements, we can assume that the person has formed a *core belief* that they cannot cope if they stray too far from home, or wander too far from the exit. In other words, they feel that their anxiety is only manageable when there is an 'escape' in view, or an escape is at least conceivable.

At some point, we may have decided that our anxiety is only manageable with the false sense of control that we think we have. People genuinely believe that they have anxiety at bay when they loiter near a fire exit, or stay within a confined radius of their homes, when all this is doing is serving to enhance anxiety's importance!

The second type of escapism is sensual. People with anxiety often try to dull or 'escape' the senses by resorting to drugs and other substances. This includes common habits like drinking alcohol, smoking marijuana, taking drugs, smoking tobacco, relying on benzodiazepines (Xanax) or sleeping tablets.

Unfortunately, and also quite sadly, people sometimes come to the assumption that anxiety is basically here to stay, therefore they resort to little 'escapes' to dull, numb or alter the senses. It is somewhat understandable.

I'd like to think that I'm no 'jobsworth' when it comes to promoting a healthy lifestyle. It would be rather hypocritical of me and it sometimes serves to put pressure on my clients. However, if we've come to rely on multiple escapes to get through the day, then I advise that we take a step back for now.

Planning around the anxiety

Of all the anxious habits associated with an anxiety disorder, this is probably the most common one. People who have built a negative association with anxiety often fall into the unhelpful habit of planning an event with anxiety at the forefront of their decision making.

Rather than planning to do something because that's what the person's rational mind wants to do, the anxious person will often factor how they *might* feel into the equation. This leads to behaviours that revolve around avoidance and escapism. To help you understand, I have listed some examples below:

- 'I've been invited to the wedding, but I'll only attend the after-party. I don't want to become anxious at the ceremony.'
- 'I want to go to the park, but I need someone to come with me.'
- 'When on holiday, I'll stay near a hospital, so they can help if something goes wrong.'
- 'I'm not looking forward to the restaurant plan with friends. I'll come home early because I'll be anxious.'
- 'If I keep myself busy then I don't have to stop and feel worried.'

What a lot of anxious people do not seem to notice is that this behaviour only serves to enhance the importance of their anxiety. It is irrational to assume that anxiety will occur, or that we can predict the future, yet we often find ourselves resigned to the 'fact' that we cannot cope in a situation, because we fully believe anxiety will intervene. This links to the notion of *core beliefs* that I'll discuss later.

The 'If I ...' plant

Another common habit of the anxious is believing in something I have coined as the *'If I ...'* plant. A large proportion of my clients at The Panic Room initially come to me with skewed preconceptions about how to manage anxiety. This usually comes in the form of reactionary behaviour that goes nowhere near the root of the problem. Let me draw upon an analogy to help me explain:

The picture above represents a plant – or a weed – that's growing through a concrete surface, such as a patio or pavement. Now, the aim of the task is to remove this weed, because in this analogy you've bizarrely become a landscape gardener. So, in order to remove the unsightly weed, we are left with two options:

1 The first option is to *temporarily* remove the weed by cutting its leaves and stem.

2 The second option is to *permanently* remove the weed by taking time to lift the concrete and work at the *root*.

It doesn't take a genius to work out that the root of the plant is anxiety itself, whilst the leaves or growth of the plant represent the *symptoms* of anxiety. Unfortunately, due to a lack of education about anxiety, many people resort to simply pruning the weed rather than removing it at its root. As you'll know, when we chop at the surface parts of a weed, it simply grows back – much like anxiety.

One of the most common behaviours of the chronically anxious is that they prune the weed of anxiety by using *'If I ...'*s, rather than addressing the problem at the root. The *'If I ...'*s represent the leaves on the diagram. People do this in an attempt to overcome their anxiety. Here are some examples below:

- 'If I eat healthily I won't be anxious. If I cut out gluten I won't be anxious. If I stop drinking alcohol, then I won't be anxious.'

- 'If I exercise every day, then I'll stop feeling anxious.'

- 'If I meditate and practise mindfulness, then I'll stop being anxious.'

- 'If I take time to explore the thoughts, maybe I can work out why I'm anxious and stop it.'

- 'If I take this miracle herb, calming tea, rescue remedy, etc., then I will stop feeling anxious.'
- 'If I take it easy, then I won't be anxious.'

All of the above are common examples that I hear from anxious people, both in my research and here at the practice. Most of the examples above actually form part of a healthy lifestyle which I do not wish to protest against. An issue occurs, however, when our expectations of this lifestyle are disproportionately high and we expect it to 'cure' us of our negative feelings. Sometimes we can end up choosing to do the above in order to *avoid* anxiety, rather than for the purpose of pursuing an overall healthy lifestyle.

By pruning *'If I ...'*s, we simply fall into the trap of enhancing anxiety's importance within our lives. The *'If I ...'* plant often characterises behaviour that focuses on avoidance and also when we *plan around the anxiety* – as mentioned in the previous subsection. The aim, however, is to remove anxiety at the *root*, so that it is effective in such a way that we need not hide our anxiety by chasing *'If I ...'*s.

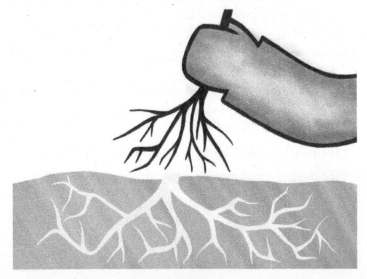

Apportioning blame for our feelings

As mentioned before, anxiety can be a confusing condition to analyse. As rational human beings, we often seek the *cause* that has produced an *effect* – something that perhaps distinguishes us from animals. This is no different when studying our own anxiety. It is ever so common for us to try to rationalise why we feel the way we do but, in doing so, we often end up with an array of conclusions that we are either not completely sure of or that are a result of pure speculation.

It is easy to pin blame for our anxiety on external factors, because it uses less energy and also takes the responsibility away from ourselves. Here are some common examples from clients (and myself) who, at one time, apportioned blame for their anxious feelings:

- 'Every time I eat a certain food, i.e. gluten, sugar, alcohol, yeast, red meat, it triggers my anxiety.'
- 'I came off antidepressants two years ago and I'm still in withdrawal. This is why I'm anxious.' (I hear this a lot.)
- 'I did recreational drugs and I feel it has broken me.'
- 'I'm anxious because of my other medical condition.'

You may have to ask yourself – is it rational for any of the above to be triggering your adrenal glands and stimulating your sympathetic nervous system? Of course, there are some external factors that may trigger anxiety, such as medication side effects, food allergies and worry stemming from taking drugs. However, I always ask clients who give statements like the above if these factors are truly responsible for their chronic feelings of anxiety.

Controlling our environment

Anxious people tend to want to control their environment because they feel they are unable to control themselves. This is usually characterised by excessive cleaning and tidying, creating endless 'to-do' lists, a constant need to feel 'productive', or manipulating other people within their environment. Often this is done subconsciously and is a result of irrational self-persuasion.

When I used to attend home call-outs for clients, I would usually walk into spotless houses. When I was anxious, my house was also really tidy; everything was symmetrical, polished and in good order. There's nothing wrong with appreciating a tidy environment, however, it is common for people with anxiety to obsess over the matter. People do this because it gives them back a sense of control, but also takes their mind away from thinking about the anxiety.

Unfortunately, this behaviour can spread into relationships. People living with someone suffering from anxiety can often have a fractious time trying to share the same environment. To the anxious person, other people around them can act like an irritant or a 'free radical'. This conflicts with the need to control their environment and sometimes can bring out the offensive side of people's personalities.

Anxiety is the centre of your life

This common habit is the one that I find the most evocative and is also something that I, myself, am no stranger to. People suffering from excessive anxiety can often make anxiety itself the centre of their universe. Their whole lives start to revolve around anxiety and its symptoms, which only serves to add to its importance.

Over time, anxiety can affect how we plan our lives, having a seat at the table in every decision-making process. This can occur with plans we make today, or even long-term goals and ambitions. What upsets me the most is that people often feel resigned to accepting anxiety will always be present, and as a result plan and live their lives accordingly. As a counsellor, I try to eradicate this *core belief* and work on changing perspectives, as well as building self-assurance.

If someone wants to do X then I believe a person should be able to do X. However, as mentioned in the section above about planning around the anxiety, people often rule out doing X and, if they do attempt to do it, it must always come with Y.

'I'm going to do X but how will Y affect me?'

The aim of this and my previous book is to build a strong understanding of anxiety and also teach self-reassurance in order to empower you to overcome the condition. Despite its many symptoms (some of which are traumatic), anxiety isn't a massively complex condition and can be overcome with a little perseverance and reflection. The remainder of this chapter will discuss practical ways you can put your anxiety into perspective.

The Anxiety Umbrella

I receive a lot of positive feedback from readers about my previous book. I was surprised, however, to hear about how much people could relate to the analogy of the Anxiety Umbrella. It has become a popular tool for helping to put anxiety into perspective. With this feedback in mind, I decided to integrate it within my counselling philosophy, so it's making another appearance here in this book.

When anxiety is high and blinding confusion has set in, you will be aware that it can be extremely difficult to prioritise, organise and focus on your 'problems' in any logical order or with any rational sense. We have so many different worries, mounting on top of our underlying worry of 'not feeling right', that we simply just don't know where to start. Have you tried waiting for the feelings to go away? You'll know it simply does not work like that.

Take a look at these examples of types of worries:

WORRIES FROM PERSPECTIVE	DAILY LIFE WORRIES	SOCIAL WORRIES	HYPOCHONDRIA (HEALTH WORRIES)
WORK/ JOB BILLS FINANCE EDUCATION DOMESTIC JOBS APPOINTMENTS SECURITY DEADLINES EXAMINATIONS UNENJOYABLE TASKS CHORES	RELATIONSHIPS FRIENDSHIPS FAMILY PARENTHOOD SOCIAL CIRCLES CONFIDENCE LOSS OF SENSE OF HUMOUR EXPECTATIONS JUDGEMENT	RELIGIOUS PERSPECTIVE PHILOSOPHICAL OUTLOOK LIFE PURPOSE SELF WORTH OVER ANALYSING SITUATIONS MISANTHROPY 'THE OUTSIDE WORLD IS A SCARY PLACE' 'NOBODY UNDERSTANDS WHAT I'M GOING THROUGH'	'AM I GOING INSANE?' SELF ANALYSING BODY CHECKING FOR PROBLEMS FEAR OF HAVING A PANIC ATTACK CONVINCED OF HAVING A HEART PROBLEM, CANCER, SCHIZOPHRENIA, ETC QUESTIONING ACHES, PAINS, TWINGES AND ASSUMING THE WORST

Now let's scatter a few examples around in the format of a thought map:

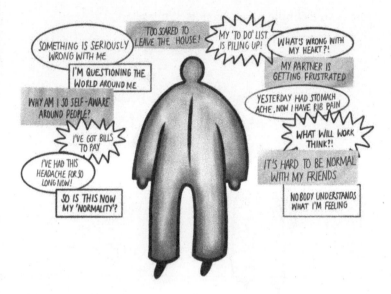

Can you see how hard it must be to prioritise a single worry to deal with? Where do we even start?

Of course, it is normal to have everyday worries such as work and social issues; however, these can soon multiply and increase in intensity when anxiety is present. Anxiety can soon act as a barrier to resolving everyday issues, which results in worries building up very quickly. Worries and stress become harder to resolve, causing an accumulation effect as expressed in the common snowball analogy.

The key here, which forms one of the core foundations of putting anxiety into perspective, is to group everything as one problem – the problem being the simplified term 'anxiety'. Take everything that you have ever assumed and worried about with regard to how you feel and throw it under a metaphorical umbrella. Label it 'anxiety' and voila – your problems are simplified into one manageable problem.

Here is an example of an Anxiety Umbrella:

As you can see, the umbrella symbolises anxiety as a whole and the 'raindrops' symbolise some of the components or symptoms that form an anxiety condition. Instead of trying to deal with every issue or symptom separately, the challenge is to try to allow all of your worries to be associated with anxiety. This not only simplifies the problem, it allows room for reflection and a point of 'blame' if life simply becomes too much.

Moving forward, it is incredibly important to see anxiety in this way. By doing this, we can begin to measure and quantify anxiety as a feeling, instead of seeing it as a plethora of individual, negative thoughts. No matter what anxious thoughts have entered the mind, we must focus on the *feelings* they evoke. Thoughts and feelings are two separate things; the focus must be on the feelings in order to make progress. This leads me to the next section, about the importance of scaling the anxiety.

The Anxiety Scale

Using this scale is not only integral to putting anxiety into perspective, but it's also a vital tool for measuring progress on your way to recovery. The Anxiety Scale is something I use with every client at The Panic Room and it has been hugely successful so far. It is a method that I have borrowed from Cognitive Behavioural Therapy (CBT), but I have manipulated it to suit anxiety specifically.

People suffer from varying degrees and types of anxiety. Some people endure frequent panic attacks, whereas others may live day to day with a general sense of unease. This is why anxiety disorders are categorised with different labels:

Types of Anxiety Disorder

- Generalised Anxiety Disorder (GAD)
- Anxiety Disorder
- Panic Disorder
- Agoraphobia
- Health Anxiety (Hypochondria)
- Social Anxiety
- Post-Traumatic Stress Disorder (PTSD)
- Obsessive Compulsive Disorder (OCD)

Regardless of what type of anxiety you have been diagnosed with, the Anxiety Scale is useful as it helps us to *quantify* our feelings. Using the concept of the Anxiety Umbrella (grouping all our worries and thoughts as one), let us look at the Anxiety Scale so we can begin to measure our anxious feelings:

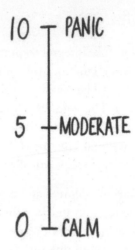

0–1 Feeling calm, relaxed and allowing the brain to wander aimlessly or focus on a point of enjoyment.

2–3 Very low-level anxiety. Almost unnoticeable. A small sense of unease or slight irritation. Mild stress.

4–5 Low-level anxiety. Feeling tense and finding it slightly difficult to relax. Tendency to focus on the negative.

6–7 Moderate anxiety. Feeling tense and apprehensive with a sense of unease. Thoughts faster than usual. Physical symptoms of anxiety noticeable. Fidgeting and strong sense of irritation. Focus on worrying thoughts.

8–9 High anxiety. Uncontrollable worry with obsessive or looping thoughts. Change in breathing, inability to keep still, prominent physical symptoms, intense feeling of dread and negative anticipation of something bad about to happen.

10 Panic attack. The feeling of complete derealisation, depersonalisation, confusion and a belief in an imminent disaster. Physical symptoms such as racing heart, difficulty breathing and sweating. Fear of a complete loss of control.

The reader should take comfort from the fact that no matter where you feel you are on the scale, nothing bad is going to happen to you. The Anxiety Scale serves to measure our anxiety, and also goes some way to measuring the amount of adrenaline that we're carrying in our bloodstream. No matter how high your anxiety score, just remember that nothing bad can happen. It is just adrenaline.

To help guide you to a sense of perspective regarding medical labels, I have put together a rough guide of anxiety levels and matched them up to the different anxiety disorders as mentioned above. This is a simplistic guide taken from experience of working with others:

GAD: A score of 3-6 throughout the day regardless.

Anxiety Disorder: A score of 6-9 throughout the day regardless.

Panic Disorder: A score of 8-10 throughout the day regardless.

Agoraphobia: A score of 1-4 inside and 6-10 outside.

Health Anxiety: A score of 3-6 in general and 6-10 when triggered by a thought.

Social Anxiety: A score of 3-5 when alone and 6-8 when in social situations (including before and after).

PTSD: 1–10 depending on thought, memory or environment.

OCD: 3-9 depending on thought, routine and associations.

Our anxiety levels are never at a constant. They will fluctuate over time and only remain high as a result of a negative thought routine. On a personal level, when I lived with panic disorder, as soon as my anxiety levels dropped, I re-enacted a thought routine which triggered my adrenaline every time I had a scary thought. I did this for years and ended up spending most of my days in a state of high anxiety, which often triggered panic attacks.

I also fell into the pitfalls, or common habits as mentioned before, that anxiety can direct you towards. The higher you are on the scale, the more likely you will catastrophise your situation. Instead of seeing that I was merely juggling adrenaline in copious amounts and, as a result, remained stuck in fight-or-flight mode – my thoughts focused in on the feelings of impending doom that panic disorder can throw at you.

The Anxiety Scale has worked so successfully because it enables clients to shift their perspective of anxiety from something they believed to be *binary* to something that can be *measurable*. Instead of throwing in the towel every time they felt anxious, my clients would focus their efforts on bringing their anxiety score down.

———————

'I'm feeling anxious at around an 8.
I'm going to try and bring this score down now.'

———————

Rather than,

———————

'Oh no, the anxiety is back again. When will it
go away?'

———————

With each increment we move down the scale, we strengthen our belief that we can make ourselves calm again. Scaling your anxiety also allows you to build up the skill of *thought observation* – something I will be discussing in the next section entitled 'Rational Mind vs Anxious Response'.

There is something very empowering in being able to bring your anxiety levels down, rather than maintaining the unrealistic expectation of trying to make it disappear altogether at the click of a finger. Sometimes we can grow very impatient with the condition, which often results in irrational behaviour, such as trying to find the 'miracle thought' or resorting to '*If I* …'s from the '*If I* …' plant.

The Loop of Peaking Anxiety

When putting anxiety into perspective, we must come to terms with the dual processes of the mind and body. We know that adrenaline is responsible for the intense, scary thoughts we have when we are anxious, so we can safely assume that if we're feeling anxious – whilst having scary thoughts – then adrenaline is the culprit. Basically, *adrenaline affects your thoughts*.

However, many people often forget that this also works in reverse – or the opposite way around. Adrenaline causes thoughts, but *thoughts* also trigger adrenaline. A negative thought can be interpreted by the body as a 'danger', thus it releases a monsoon of adrenaline to help you defend against the thought.

This brings me back to the sympathetic nervous system. If this system is overstimulated, then our bodies are prone to releasing disproportionate amounts of adrenaline at any given moment.

For example, we could be walking through a park with a level of 3 on the Anxiety Scale, and suddenly experience a negative thought. The body then interprets this as a danger, and releases more adrenaline, pushing our anxiety level up to an 8. We then feel scared and anxious. However, the mind and body want to know why there's so much adrenaline on board, therefore we begin to explore yet more negative thoughts. These negative thoughts are caused by the adrenaline. Therefore, in this example, you've got both thoughts caused by adrenaline and adrenaline caused by thoughts.

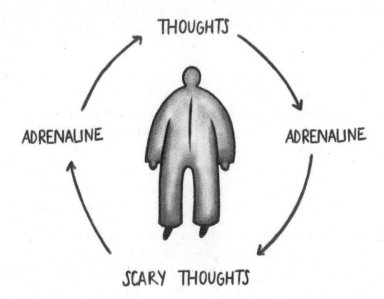

This process can easily cause a 'loop' of negative thoughts and feelings. People with anxiety and panic disorder will often find themselves exploring thoughts caused by adrenaline which, in turn, triggers yet more adrenaline, which then sources yet more thoughts. I have coined this phenomenon the 'Loop of Peaking Anxiety' – a term that may already be familiar to you.

Let us look at how the Loop of Peaking Anxiety is represented using our Anxiety Scale:

ANXIETY AND THE PEAK

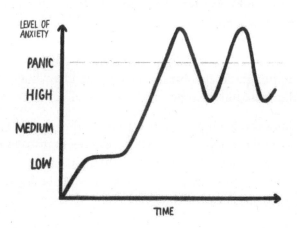

This graph represents someone who suffers from Panic Disorder. The pattern of fluctuations you can see would be similar for other anxiety conditions, the only difference being the overall levels of anxiety. The person with Panic Disorder seems to get stuck at a high level of anxiety and panic; the anxiety score stays in the 'high' bracket of 8–10. This is the Loop of Peaking Anxiety.

The reason why people get stuck in the Loop of Peaking Anxiety is because they fail to see that the thoughts are harmless and that they are simply a result of excess adrenaline. Rather than thinking, *'Oh, I'm thinking and feeling that a disaster is about to happen again. It's OK because I know this is adrenaline'*, people are often easily persuaded by the thoughts because they're accompanied by strong feelings of unease. Furthermore, they may lack the skill of self-reassurance, something I have discovered through working with people at The Panic Room.

The Anxiety Scale is an incredibly helpful tool for measuring our progress. It also allows us to break down anxiety into manageable chunks. As mentioned near the beginning of the book, the ultimate goal is to calm the sympathetic nervous system. By doing this, we prevent the body from releasing ridiculous amounts of adrenaline every time we have a disturbing thought. It also breaks the loop of adrenaline causing thoughts and thoughts causing adrenaline.

I cannot stress enough how helpful it is to visualize your anxiety in this way, with the hope that I can convey how to manage and overcome your anxiety using the successful approach I use with my clients. It starts by simplifying, quantifying and putting it all into an understandable perspective.

Summary and Step Two

Step One looked at understanding anxiety by considering it as a feeling, as well the biological components responsible for the feelings. In this section, we looked at how we can put anxiety into some much-needed perspective.

Firstly, see if you can relate to any of the common habits of the anxious. It is ever so common for people to resort to catastrophising and believing in the '*What if?*'s that adrenaline and the mind can conjure. If these are present in your life, then it will be no surprise to you if you have reacted to these thoughts by altering your behaviours.

Please take time out to reflect on whether you rely on avoidance or escapism in your day-to-day life. Perhaps you can identify with the '*If I …*' plant, or maybe you've fallen into the habit of apportioning blame to external factors? Furthermore, if anxiety has been the focal point of your life for a significant amount of time, rest assured that you are allowed to take a step back. Anxiety doesn't need to be the centre of your universe any more, as this only serves to enhance its importance. Remember that anxiety is just a matter of adrenaline and a stimulated sympathetic nervous system. Your rational mind knows this, despite the array of disturbing thoughts you've had to endure.

We must simplify our world of worries by focusing on anxiety itself – not the individual thoughts that plague us. We can do this by using the Anxiety Umbrella. Let us group all our worries and concerns together and label the whole thing 'anxiety'. Doing this allows us to focus our attention on the quantifiable *feeling* of anxiety. This is where the true problem lies.

Once we have formed a perspective on what we are focusing on, we must begin scaling the anxiety. The Anxiety Scale helps us to visualize the anxiety and also allows us to measure it in a given situation. The scale also allows us to see anxiety from a non-binary viewpoint – taking us away from viewing it as something that is either 'there' or 'not there'.

Start by scaling your anxiety right now. Then scale it again at times when you are anxious, but also at times when you are calm. Begin to identify that anxiety can occur and disappear depending on the situation or environment, or in response to a particular thought.

I write this after seeing a client who came into the practice with anxiety at a 6. By the end of the session she measured her anxiety at a 3. Although the anxiety hadn't disappeared, she took huge encouragement from being able to bring the level down herself. This is something I wish the anxious readers of this book to replicate for themselves.

PART 3

Understanding the Anxious Mind

Rational Mind vs Anxious Response

We're going to move on to exploring exactly *why* the mind focuses on scary, irrational thoughts when we find ourselves excessively anxious. By doing this, we can learn the skill of observing thoughts, which will go a significant way towards helping us take our mind away from them.

Anxiety always causes an internal dialogue within our thought process. You may or may not be aware of it but, when we are anxious, there are two voices playing in our minds. The first voice is the *rational mind*. This is the voice that uses logic, pragmatism and the balance of probability when weighing up choices. Basically, when we are calm, the rational mind has full control over our thoughts and decisions. For the purpose of simplification, we can call this the 'normal' mind that operates day to day and thrives in a secure and safe environment.

There is, however, an added dialogue when we find ourselves anxious. If we find ourselves in fight-or-flight mode, or anywhere above a 2 on our anxiety scale, the *anxious response* always seems to chime in with its two cents regarding any situation. You know if the anxious response has had an input when you are entertaining thoughts that begin with '*What if?*'.

You must remember that the anxious response is something that is there to protect us. However, in my and many other experts' opinions, the anxious response has failed to evolve and adapt to the rapid societal evolution of modern times. As a result of this, people living with anxiety have to endure all sorts of '*What if?*'s in contexts where this primitive response is, arguably, redundant.

When we find ourselves high on our anxiety scales, we must take into account that the anxious response will explore the dangers and '*What if?*'s of a given situation. This is incredibly important to distinguish and will contribute to empowering your skill of thought observation.

Here are some common examples of internal dialogue between the *rational mind* and the *anxious response*:

Scenario 1

A person is about to board a train.

Rational Mind: You are boarding this train in order to reach your destination quickly and efficiently.

Anxious Response: *What if you become anxious on the train and cannot escape?*

Scenario 2

A person is worried about their anxiety and how they are currently feeling.

Rational Mind: You are anxious because you keep triggering fight-or-flight mode. Your nervous system is overstimulated and you are in a bad thought habit.

Anxious Response: *What if this is something worse? What if this is a serious mental condition? What if you lose control at any moment?*

Scenario 3

A person has been invited to a party by an old friend. However, they have not been out to a social gathering for a long time.

Rational Mind: It will be nice to see your old friend and seize the opportunity to meet new people. You've not been to a party in ages!

Anxious Response: *What if you become anxious in front of people? What if your friend recognises you are different? What if you embarrass yourself? What if you need to escape? What if you postpone and come back to it when you're feeling 'better'?*

Scenario 4

A person is experiencing symptoms of IBS such as bloating, discomfort, mixed stools and abdominal pains. They are also feeling anxious.

Rational Mind: Your body is prioritising excessive adrenaline at the moment. Therefore, the digestive cycle is temporarily disturbed. You're eating poorly, too.

Anxious Response: *What if you have developed an allergy to a certain food? What if you have a digestion problem? What if you have a serious condition, such as cancer?*

Scenario 5

A person is planning a holiday with their family.

Rational Mind: A holiday will be a nice opportunity for you and your family to have a fun, relaxing break.

Anxious Response: *What if you have a panic attack on the way? What if you become inconsolable on the plane? What if you need to escape back home, but can't? What could happen if you have to drive with your loved ones in the car?*

The important point to remember here is that the more anxious you are, then the 'louder' the anxious response becomes. In other words, the higher you are on the Anxiety Scale, the more prominent the anxious response seems to be when weighing up a decision.

Sometimes my clients find it useful to picture the rational mind discussing options with the anxious response at a table – the rational mind pitching ideas and then listening to counter-arguments provided by the anxious response. By doing this, we can observe that, in most scenarios (similar to the examples) the anxious response is not needed.

This is not to say that the anxious response is useless, however. When we are rational and faced with actual danger, it actually comes in quite handy. Look at this example:

Scenario 6

A person comes face to face with a rabid, aggressive dog bracing itself for attack.

Rational Mind: Get the hell out of here or fight.

Anxious Response: *Get the hell out of here or fight!*

The key here is to silence the anxious response in 'normal' situations. This is the same as bringing our anxiety scale down to low levels. If we fail to do this, then it increases our chances of developing self-perpetuating anxiety symptoms.

With excessive anxiety, it is important to keep reminding yourself that the mind and body want to know *why* there is so much adrenaline on board. This is why we can so often get carried away with thoughts and end up in situations where our thoughts appear to be in a constant loop (the Loop of Peaking Anxiety).

Personally, I find it no surprise that people end up catastrophising self-perpetuating symptoms. The mind and body, as well as the anxious response, try to help you 'work out' why you feel the way you do by providing you with

possible answers and solutions. For example, if we have
a headache, but are anxious, we could easily spend time
entertaining thoughts about our headache being worse
than it actually is. Furthermore, if we feel anxious, whilst
acknowledging the fact that we have felt anxious for a long
time, we may well end up entertaining catastrophic thoughts
about our state of well-being.

Self-perpetuating anxiety symptoms

Here is a list of the common, self-perpetuating symptoms I
hear of from clients:

- **The headache** – person has a prolonged headache. This
  headache is then worried about. Adrenaline causes the
  headache to become worse. The Anxious Mind concludes
  that it is a brain tumor.
- **The IBS** – person has digestion problems. Person tries
  to fix it through medication and changing diet. Problems
  still remain because of adrenaline and other chemicals.
  The Anxious Mind suggests it is a stomach ulcer or
  something worse.
- **The muscle twitching** – person has muscle twitching
  and cramps. Person worries about the symptom, which
  causes more adrenaline and cortisol. This makes the
  twitching and the obsession more prominent. The
  Anxious Mind suggests that it is multiple sclerosis or
  Motor Neurone Disease (MND).
- **Heart palpitations** – person has heart palpitations and
  increased heartbeat. This symptom is worried about, thus
  releasing more adrenaline. This also triggers IBS, which
  is linked to palpitations. Palpitations continue and the
  Anxious Mind assumes there is a problem with the heart.

And perhaps the most common of them all:

- **The unexplained anxiety** – person has prolonged anxiety and cannot decipher why. Person then worries about their own state of mental health, thus causing yet more excessive adrenaline. The anxious mind tries to help by providing answers and solutions, with the person resorting to trying to find the 'miracle thought' or an easily identifiable cause. Over time, the Anxious Mind assumes that we have a serious mental health condition.

The anxious response – or 'anxious mind' when considering internal dialogue – is responsible when we perceive common anxiety symptoms as something far worse. It provides the '*What if?*' that can be difficult to let go of when we find ourselves high on the anxiety scale.

The key skill to develop here is to acknowledge that your thinking is not balanced if you find yourself anxious. When we acknowledge this, we can learn to let the thoughts pass through the mind without making our overall anxiety any worse. Furthermore, by observing the anxious thoughts and then choosing to ignore them, we allow the body to calm more quickly than usual.

With regard to being in an anxious state, always keep in mind that there are two narratives at play. The more we choose to adhere to the suggestions provided by the rational mind, the more we quieten the anxious response. This will make more sense throughout the book.

The three core statements of anxiety

At the heart of anxiety lie three *core statements* that define the actions and behaviours of people living with an anxiety condition. These core statements act as a precursor to our thoughts when weighing up decisions in an anxious state. Referring to the previous section, these three statements are almost always used by the anxious mind or anxious response when pitching a 'danger' to the rational mind. It is because of these statements that we often choose to avoid, escape or run away from situations and scenarios. I often term these statements 'The Voice of Anxiety'.

'What if ...?'

The first statement is something that we have been introduced to already: the '*What if*'. The '*What if*' usually occurs when we are already anxious. As explained before, the higher our anxiety scales, then the stronger – or louder – this seems to become. For example, if we find ourselves at an 8 on the anxiety scale, then we are probably dealing with an overabundance of '*What if*'s.

We don't already need to be in a situation to experience the '*What if*' of anxiety. In fact, it usually manifests itself when contemplating a decision. If we choose to avoid an activity because we fear for our well-being, then it is because we have listened to several '*What if*'s during the decision-making process. Ultimately, we have placed importance on the anxious mind saying '*What if X?*', or '*What if Y happens?*' before making our final decision. If you have ever received Cognitive Behavioural Therapy, then you may be familiar with this term.

'I can't ...'

With regard to anxiety, the term '*I can't ...*' is an example of a *negative core belief*. A core belief is something that we have concluded about ourselves and our ability to cope with anxiety in a given situation. I discuss the concept of core beliefs throughout this book.

The '*I can't* ...' is often characterised by the immediate dismissal of a practical idea. Here are some examples I have taken from working with clients at The Panic Room:

Therapist: Why don't you just go ahead and book the flights?

Client: I can't fly because of how I am.

Therapist: Have you considered just going to the event and seeing what happens?

Client: I can't even leave my house!

Therapist: You are allowed to be anxious for your presentation. Why not have a go?

Client: No way; I can't ...

An '*I can't* ...' is an assumption of how we will deal with an event that hasn't even happened yet. It is actually an insight into how we view ourselves and our ability to cope with stress. It is also, quite sadly, an indicator that we may have lost hope with regard to tackling our anxiety condition.

I like to slowly eradicate these '*I can't* ...'s at my practice by setting small targets and positively reflecting on achievements. By doing this, clients can begin to erode the negative core beliefs that they may possess about their lack of inner resources.

I suggest looking at things that you immediate dismiss in your life. If you assume that you are unable to do them, then you may be abiding by one of the core statements of anxiety. '*I can't* ...'s are life-hindering because they prevent us from getting out of the door and attempting to tackle anxiety. The sooner we identify and challenge them, the sooner we can progress with overcoming the condition.

'I should …'

The phrase '*I should* …' is perhaps the most common, yet unnoticed, core statement of anxiety and is heavily associated with Generalised Anxiety Disorder (GAD). On a personal note, I really enjoy exploring '*I should* …'s with clients, as it can prove to be a real eye-opener with regard to anxious habits and routines.

If we find ourselves living out our daily lives with mild to moderate anxiety (3–6 using our scale), we may often find that we can function, but with an ever-present feeling of moderate fear or dread. To address this fear, many people misinterpret the feeling as a guilty urge to do something 'productive' as an attempt to ignore the feeling of anxiety, or to make it go away.

This is the birth of the '*I should* …' statement. It is characterised by an over-zealous emphasis on completing tasks, implementing order and controlling an environment. One of the most common behaviours dictated by an '*I should* …' is the need to constantly clean and do chores. Further to this, traits similar to OCD can be present, as people like to abide by checklists or 'to-do' lists. Many of these mental to-do lists are never-ending.

There is nothing wrong with enjoying cleaning, tidying or living with a sense of structured organisation. However, the behaviour can often be exaggerated and turn into an 'escape' rather than the completion of a necessary task.

Of course, '*I should* …' isn't exclusive to behaviours within the home that revolve around cleaning and a sense of order. '*I should* …'s can stretch into all aspects of our lives – particularly our careers – and can often prevent us from stopping and living in the present moment. It is ever so

I SHOULD...

common for an '*I should* ...' to stretch into existential thinking, which can often convince us that the future can make us happy more than the present.

Furthermore, this can often present a barrier to positive self-reflection. When we achieve something in our daily lives, we are allowed to take a moment to reflect on that achievement. However, an '*I should* ...' often causes us to 'move the goalposts' – as soon as we have achieved something, suddenly the next task becomes the priority, so we end up chasing a never-ending goal that ultimately never satiates us.

Perhaps most importantly, an '*I should* ...' acts as a barrier to simply stopping and relaxing. During prolonged bouts of anxiety, the parasympathetic nervous system is screaming out to be activated through rest, relaxation and enjoyment. However, people with anxiety can easily slip into bad habits revolving around arduous tasks – forever chasing a level of contentment that they feel they can achieve through excessive organisation of their environment.

Take a moment to reflect on how many of your actions are influenced by an '*I should …*' statement. Note them down and bear them in mind as we progress through the book. Furthermore, try to acknowledge the other core statements of anxiety: the '*What if*'s and the '*I can't* …'s.

The three stages of 'fight or flight'

In order to understand the anxious mind, we have to further understand how it acts under the influence of adrenaline. We have understood, thus far, that when we have to live with excessive adrenaline, the mind and body want to know *why* the extra adrenaline is on board – particularly when we are high on our anxiety scales. This then triggers a cascade of different thoughts as the mind forages to find out where the 'danger' is. It is the process of finding this danger that I want to share with you in this section.

When we find ourselves experiencing high levels of anxiety, then we know that we are experiencing the excessive adrenaline that's roaming around our body. The anxious mind (fight or flight) then tries to work out *why* all of this extra adrenaline is present. It does this by exploring three different areas to find the 'danger' that matches why we feel the way we do. We can also observe this as three different stages. I have outlined the stages below:

Stage 1: Our environment

The first place the anxious mind tries to find the 'danger' is within our immediate environment. Try to visualize the fight-or-flight response scrambling to match up dangers to the current level of adrenaline by scanning for these dangers within our environment. This is the primitive version of the fight-or-flight response and goes back to prehistory when we were hunter-gatherers.

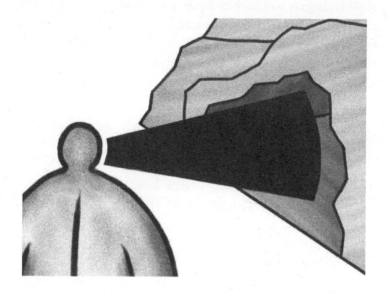

You can see why scanning the environment in prehistoric times could have been helpful. Having an adrenal response that helps us immediately scan the environment for danger is a useful safety mechanism, especially if faced with sabre-tooth tigers and other beasts of the prehistoric world. However, as modern society has developed, the need for this response has declined. We live in comparatively safe times but, as mentioned above, many people believe that parts of the anxious response haven't caught up with the economic 'evolution' of the human race. Worries become more focused on things we cannot see, such as bank statements and careers, rather than immediate, physical threats around us.

Basically, in times of excessive anxiety, the mind scans the environment first. This is done within a fraction of a second and is a natural, innate response. Sometimes, the anxious mind can interpret dangers within the environment. These dangers aren't necessarily rational, but they can be interpreted as dangers all the same. A large proportion of people with anxiety will not identify dangers within their immediate environment. However, people with agoraphobia and social anxiety can often get caught out. Here are some common examples of the anxious response finding dangers in our immediate environment:

SOCIAL ANXIETY

- 'The person over there thinks ill of me. What if they are talking about me?'
- 'My colleague gave me a strange look. What if I have done something wrong?'
- 'I have to sit around people and speak up. What if I'm judged?'

AGORAPHOBIA

- 'I am stood outside and I am extremely anxious. Therefore it is being outside that is the danger.'
- 'I am in my home, but I get anxious at the thought of leaving when I look through my window. The outside has too many "What if's."'
- 'There is a lock on the door; what if I cannot escape?' (Claustrophobia)

These are simple examples to explain how the anxious mind looks to the environment first for reasons to explain our anxiety. This may or may not apply to you, but it is worth learning about in order to gain a greater understanding of how anxiety works.

Stage 2: Scanning ourselves

The second way the anxious mind scans for dangers is by focusing upon the body. This is where a lot of clients with health anxiety (hypochondria) get blindsided. Once (if) the anxious mind has decided that no dangers lie within the environment, it then turns its attention inward, by performing a full sweep of the body in search of any potential faults.

This is why people can often convince themselves that they have something catastrophically wrong with them. The anxious mind can often stop its scan on a physical symptom of anxiety, such as heart palpitations, headaches, abdominal pains, dizziness and lethargy. However, because the anxiety is excessive, this affects our response to the suggestions that the anxious mind provides. Take this for example:

Sarah is sat in her bedroom. She currently has a high level of anxiety which lies at around an 8 on her anxiety scale. The anxious mind is confused, because this is Sarah's bedroom and there usually isn't any danger here. However, the anxious mind cares about Sarah, so it tries to help her discover where the danger lies. After all, she must be anxious for a reason!

The anxious mind then conducts a thorough search of the body from head to toe. If you are a self-aware person, you may have caught yourself doing this – trying to find out what's 'wrong' with you. With health anxiety, the anxious mind likes to focus on any aches, pains or incongruities that the body may be experiencing. Once these have been found, they are often focused upon, then subsequently catastrophised.

Sarah's anxious mind concludes that the danger is not within her bedroom, so it shifts and begins to scan her body. Sarah notices she has had a headache for a few days now, as well as feeling lightheaded. Despite knowing that this is probably the result of stress, her anxious mind has other ideas. 'This must be cancer or an aneurism,' her anxious mind concludes. Further to this, she notices she has had pains in her stomach and ribs. 'The cancer has spread, Sarah,' suggests her anxious mind. Sarah becomes even more anxious as a result, which leads to a continuation of the current symptoms.

Sarah is susceptible to health anxiety and therefore begins to listen to her anxious mind when it suggests that her headache is the immediate danger. I have noticed that people who have been exposed to illness or bereavement are susceptible to health anxiety. Furthermore, we are surrounded by constant information about serious illnesses, besides the likelihood that we may know someone who has passed away prematurely.

If you are susceptible to bouts of health anxiety, then please acknowledge that the anxious mind has scoured the body and focused upon this. Just remind yourself that the thoughts are more than likely to be extremely disproportionate to the actual truth of the situation. Remember to listen to the rational mind and focus on what it has to say.

During the body scan, the anxious mind can force us to catastrophise about other aspects of our health that go beyond physical symptoms. We can begin to focus on how we feel psychologically as a symptom. Basically, we can start to worry about why we are worrying; the anxious mind can identify the process of worrying as a danger in itself! If you have ever woken up in the morning and immediately analysed how you feel, this is an example of this tendency.

Remember that not only does the anxious mind scan the body physically, it also scans us emotionally. This can lead to the unnecessary catastrophisation of negative feelings, and often provokes fears of developing incurable mental health conditions. I can't tell you the number of anxious people I have worked with at The Panic Room who thought they were 'going insane'. Some examples of emotion scanning include worrying about tiredness, depression, brain fog, sadness and worry itself.

Not everyone gets caught out by the second stage of the fight-or-flight response. It is common for people to quickly elude the first two stages, which leads us on to discussing the third and final stage. This is the last place where the anxious mind looks for danger before giving up!

Stage 3: Time travelling

The third and final place the anxious mind forages for dangers is within our memories. As a result of this, we can become stuck dwelling on and blaming ourselves for things we have done in the past as the cause for how we feel, or we could spend time predicting dangers in the future. If the anxious mind concludes that the danger does not lie within ourselves or the environment, then it searches for danger by exploring our memories. It is this third stage of the adrenaline response that I have named 'time travelling', as it deals with dangers that lie outside the present moment.

Let us take the past as an example and see how it affects our rationalisation during anxious moments. I will draw upon some common examples that I have heard in my practice:

TIME TRAVELLING: THE PAST

- 'I'm anxious because I have done myself damage in some way.'
- 'I'm anxious because of something I ate.'

- 'I'm anxious because I offended a colleague.'
- 'I'm anxious because I did not tidy up.'
- 'I'm anxious because I have pushed myself too far.'

These are some examples from clients and people I have studied during my research. Remember that these thoughts arrive almost instantaneously – a fraction of a second after the anxious mind concludes that there is no danger within the environment or within our bodies. Sometimes this kind of rummaging of the memory can lead to mental fixations which, in turn, create irrational associations with certain things. This is why people can develop traits similar to OCD, where any current anxiety is linked and associated to a particular action not being performed in the past.

It is very important to remember that the anxious mind makes assumptions about the future based on our memories. Again, I will provide some examples from experience:

TIME TRAVELLING: THE FUTURE

- 'Last time I was anxious something bad happened, therefore something bad is going to happen again.'
- 'I keep being anxious, therefore I might break very soon.'
- 'Something bad is about to happen. It's not happening now, but it is about to happen. I can sense it.'
- 'I'm either going to collapse, faint, have a heart attack or simply drop dead. Something of this severity is about to happen.'
- 'I feel like this person is going to reprimand me about something.'

The third stage of fight or flight relies on speculation to thrive. This is why many people become confused about the condition and often become stuck in an anxious habit. One of the biggest stumbling blocks in overcoming anxiety is allowing yourself to separate thoughts and feelings; it may be helpful to observe the mind frantically searching for dangers via the three stages set out in this section and, as a result, distance yourself from the frightening thoughts that the anxious mind can conjure.

The irrational, scary thoughts that anxious people endure on a daily basis are a product of the process laid out in this section. I reiterate that they are merely a product of the anxious mind trying to match up scary thoughts and scenarios that match the current level of adrenaline in the body. This is why I urge people to start scaling their anxiety.

Low-level anxiety can conjure thoughts such as forgetting to lock the door, leaving the iron on or wondering if we have received a parking ticket; whereas high levels of anxiety can produce frightening thoughts which are proportionate to the level of adrenaline we are processing. Such thoughts include ruminating about instant disaster, impending doom, hopelessness and even death. Whatever the thoughts, just remember that they are all a result of the same three-stage process.

The Gear Analogy

A very popular tool to use when trying to understand and calm the anxious mind is something I have termed the Gear Analogy. This analogy is extremely useful because it helps us to highlight how unbalanced our days are in terms of work, play and rest. I define 'work' as how hard our brains are working, as well as how much physical activity we put ourselves through. A healthy lifestyle will have a nice balance of all three – something that is scarce in almost every person with an anxiety condition.

The Gear Analogy is particularly beneficial for people whose lives are dictated by the '*I should* …'s and '*What if* …'s mentioned previously. It also applies to the notion of escapism. People who act out of the constant need to feel 'productive', or who are looking for an instant fix to mend how they feel, should pay close attention to this section and apply it to their lives.

The Gear Analogy is simple. If you think of a car with a manual gearbox, it usually has five gears (excluding reverse). In this analogy, we are represented by the car and the gears represent the different speeds at which we can operate. In order to live a healthy lifestyle and get up to speed efficiently, we need to make efficient use of *all* the gears. First gear represents rest, fun and tranquillity, whereas fifth gear represents a high level of brain activity, as well as physical exertion.

The gears can mostly be defined by the individual as they apply to their own lives. However, I have included a rough outline below in order to give a general sense of what they entail:

FIRST GEAR

Being in first gear revolves around mental and physical relaxation. This is usually found in activities that are positively immersive, such as reading, watching television, laughing, meditating and being mindful of our surroundings. Ultimately, first gear is when we find ourselves in the moment and achieving relaxation.

First gear scares a lot of people because it often forces people to confront their thoughts and feelings. First gear requires us to stop, reflect and be open to entertaining thoughts and feelings, as well as being open to other mixed emotions. First gear is also easily achieved when we do not fear boredom. Almost everyone who lives with excessive anxiety will be living with a scarcity of first-gear activities.

SECOND GEAR

Second gear is similar to first gear but usually entails some mild physical activity or positive stimulation. For example, you could be enjoying a radio show whilst doing the ironing, or listening to music whilst on a brisk walk. You can also be sitting down whilst in second gear, but your mind could still be stimulated by something that triggers the emotions, such as partaking in a heated debate, or watching comedy or action films.

THIRD GEAR

Third gear is characterised by lots of physical activity or putting the mind through mild stress. At work – perhaps during a good day – we will probably operate in third gear as we are required to use our minds and we may be on our feet a little bit. Third gear can be identified when you acknowledge that you are in 'work mode' and willing to get stuff done!

Third gear can also be channelled into healthy activity such as running, swimming or an intense gym session. It is helpful to be in this gear in terms of motivation, but becomes a problem when we don't know how to shift down the gears into relaxation.

FOURTH GEAR

Fourth gear could be characterised by a busy day at work, or frantically organising with moderate stress levels. This gear is usually saved for our most productive time of the day when workload is at a maximum. Fourth gear often finds us on our feet and expending a lot of physical energy.

Furthermore, fourth gear often represents times when we are anxious – particularly with generalised anxiety. Many people living with anxiety will often find themselves in fourth gear in scenarios where they simply don't need to be. Being in this gear strongly links to the '*I should* ...'s and the need to feel productive, as I have mentioned previously.

I have found that a lot of people turn to exercise as a means of ignoring the fact that they struggle to shift down from fourth gear. A disproportionate number of clients I have worked with have placed huge focus on activities such as the gym, marathons, triathlons or constant house renovation.

Although not applicable to everyone with anxiety (as these activities could just be of general interest), I still like to link these activities to the '*If I* …'s discussed previously. I have observed, on many occasions, that activities are often used as an excuse to ignore fourth gear and the anxiety that comes with it.

FIFTH GEAR

Fifth gear is engaged when the body goes through high levels of physical and mental exertion. Imagine how teachers behave the night before an inspection, or doctors and nurses in response to an emergency. Fifth gear also represents high amounts of anxiety – including panic attacks.

Operating in fifth gear is perfectly healthy as long as it is balanced with low-gear activity. If we are spending most of each day oscillating between third and fifth gear, then it's highly likely that we'll be susceptible to experiencing excessive anxiety.

It is possible to be stuck in the higher gears without moving, as high amounts of anxiety can cause us to overthink even when sitting in a chair. This is still physically exhausting, as the body has a higher heart rate, muscle tension and fight-or-flight hormones to process.

In my previous book, I stated that the working cogs of your anxiety were set in motion way before you began to notice it. One of the main 'cogs' can be highlighted using the Gear Analogy. For example, if you have spent time worrying, frantically organising, chasing '*If I* …'s and '*I should* …'s, ruminating about health, loved ones and lifestyle problems, then it would be safe to assume that this is valuable time taken away from being in first gear.

Shifting down the gears is essential to calming the sympathetic nervous system and activating the parasympathetic. Spending too much time in the higher gears – without adequate rest – leaves us open to dealing with excessive adrenaline in times when we simply do not need it. You can observe that people who take time out to rest can deal with stress and workload easily and efficiently.

Summary and Step Three

Part 3 of this book has looked at how we can *understand* the anxious mind. In order to do this, we must first distinguish the *anxious* mind from the *rational* mind. We must learn to observe the internal dialogue that occurs between the rational mind and the anxious mind. This was covered in the first section, entitled 'Rational Mind vs Anxious Response'.

Remember that the anxious mind loves '*What if?*'s and seemingly becomes louder and more convincing the higher we find ourselves on our anxiety scale. Within this internal dialogue between rational and anxious mind, there are *three core statements* that seem to arise – particularly if the anxious mind is listened to on a frequent basis. These statements start with:

1 What if ...?

2 I should ...

3 I can't ...

Please take some time to step back and observe your thought process when making decisions. Try to identify whether your behaviour is heavily influenced by the three core statements of anxiety. I always advocate the use of a journal, or any way in which you can record/observe thoughts.

Further to this, we can identify what our anxious mind likes to highlight as 'dangers' when we find ourselves in 'fight-or-flight' mode. To help you identify the flagged dangers, you can break down the fight-or-flight response into the *three stages of adrenaline*. These stages are:

1 Scanning the environment

2 Scanning the body

3 Scanning our memories and making presumptions.

The anxious response is universal across all variations (or diagnoses) of anxiety disorder. It is extremely useful to acknowledge where your anxiety manifests and focuses its attention. For example, a tendency for the anxious mind to find 'dangers' within the environment seems to be paramount with people who are agoraphobic or suffer from claustrophobia. Health anxiety is synonymous with interpreting dangers when scanning the body, while a whole plethora of diagnoses are associated with finding dangers in the past or predicting dangers in the future.

Reflecting on our daily thoughts and behaviours using the *Gear Analogy*, we can begin to see how potential habits have arisen over time that have catered to anxiety. At The Panic Room, I always stress the importance of finding activities that help clients spend more time in first and second gear. Usually people avoid these gears because they are afraid to face their thoughts and feelings when they stop being active. Please take time to observe how you operate throughout your day. In my experience, I have observed that almost everyone who lives with excessive anxiety spends little to no time in first gear.

PART 4

Training the Rational Mind

Core beliefs

I have found that one of the most important factors in recovering from an anxiety condition is constructing and utilising a strong *core belief*. A core belief is a concept that I have pinched from CBT and have found it to be invaluable both in practice and in my personal life.

A core belief is something that we believe in regardless of how anxious we may be. For example, we may believe that the sky is blue; we would believe this whether we were calm or on the verge of a panic attack. Therefore, we can safely state that one of our core beliefs is that the sky is blue, despite how anxious we may be feeling.

I have often found, however, that the highly anxious rely on a system based on *temporary*, rather than core, beliefs. For example, when a person with health anxiety is calm, they may conclude that any ailments or symptoms they notice are merely the result of something mundane. They may not believe that a headache or a stomach ache is the result of something serious and that, overall, they are 'OK'.

However, when the person with health anxiety presents as anxious, the belief that they are 'OK' can quickly dissipate. If they are anxious, then the anxious mind may speculate that they have something more serious, like a brain tumor or a serious stomach illness. The conviction that they are 'OK' disappears because they abided by a *temporary* belief. Suddenly the person may start ruminating about their symptoms and whirling up into a panic. It is important to note that this same principle can be applied to other forms of anxiety, such as agoraphobia, panic disorder, driving anxiety, social anxiety and so on. Basically, when we start feeling like our anxiety is dangerous, we have lost the temporary belief that we're 'OK'.

This is why the role of a *core belief* is so important. If we can somehow convince ourselves that strange feelings, intrusive thoughts and recurring anxiety symptoms are the result of 'just anxiety', then we can begin to establish a core belief. Ultimately, by believing that we're 'OK' regardless of how high our anxiety may be, we can work on bringing it back down again. I will draw upon the use of the *Anxiety Scale* and some hypothetical examples to put this into context:

1 Let's say we wake up on a Saturday and we feel calm; our anxiety is a 1 or a 2 on our anxiety scale and we feel like going out for a walk in the sunshine. On some days, we feel anxious and don't feel like we can cope outside, but today we feel like leaving the house because we feel good. So, we end up stepping out of the front door and walking to our favourite woodland.

2 As we are walking, we suddenly feel a little uneasy and our anxiety rises to a 5 or a 6 on the scale. All of a sudden, we don't seem to feel comfortable on the walk and we begin to question our ability to cope with where we are.

3 Our anxiety rises further to an 8, which gives rise to
   anxious thoughts (such as '*What if*'s) and scenarios created
   by adrenaline and the anxious mind.

4 We eventually decide that, in order to feel safe, we must
   turn back and go home.

Ultimately, the temporary belief – that helped us go on the
walk in the first place – seemed to dissolve as soon as we felt
anxious. This applies to many situations, from social anxiety to
a general worry about any event.

If, however, we possessed a strong *core belief* that we would be
alright regardless of how we felt in the woods, we would have
continued the walk and given the brain and body the chance
to ease the anxiety. By continuing, we could have told the
anxious brain that there was no danger, which is like telling
it not to release as much adrenaline in the future. Eventually
the anxiety measured on our scale would have slowly come
down. I feel it is a result of habit that we are prevented from
establishing strong core beliefs.

Remember, anxiety is *just anxiety* and the feeling itself
cannot hurt you. By reminding ourselves of this and,
through our behaviours, showing that we're sticking by
this belief, then we can begin to build a core belief that
can support us again and again.

Much like many of my clients, I was someone who
experienced multiple 'panic attacks' per day and was a living
example of a person devoid of any healthy core beliefs. Each
panic attack was a terrifying reminder that made me feel like
I could lose control or drop dead at any moment. I can safely
say, however, that I have not had a panic attack for many years.
My anxiety rarely creeps past a 5 on the scale, and I would
deem this normal anxiety in any case. This is all down to the
fact that whenever I feel any anxiety rising, I can refer to my

own personal belief that I am 'OK' – I know what anxiety and adrenaline feel like and I believe to my 'core' that nothing bad will happen to me. This is what I try to teach to clients in my practice. Once we realise, or believe, that a panic attack cannot 'harm' us, then we can establish a core belief that helps to cushion us when we feel our anxiety rising. Behaviour and habits play a huge part in all of this.

Changing our habits

A habit is defined as a behaviour pattern acquired by frequent repetition, which a person knowingly or unknowingly practises on a recurrent basis. At my practice, I spend a lot of time discussing habits with clients to teach them just how integral they are to the functioning of any anxiety condition.

The term 'habit' comes with an abundance of negative connotations. It is often associated with unhealthy lifestyle choices or used to point out irregular behaviour. For example, you could be in a bad habit of smoking at certain times, drinking inappropriately, or forgetting to take the bins out. Habits, however, are not necessarily a bad thing; they exist to help our days run more smoothly.

Habits exist because they save the brain time and energy in many common scenarios. You will notice the positive results of habits when you complete actions seemingly on 'auto-pilot'. Think about it: how much did you really concentrate on brushing your teeth this morning? How consciously aware are you when changing gear or using the indicators in a car? Perhaps someone asked you how you were this afternoon and you responded with the obligatory, *'I'm fine thanks, how are you?'*

You will find that a large proportion of your day runs according to habit. From opening doors or sitting in the same chair to eating a meal in a certain way and, even, greeting people. Even walking is the result of habit! Ultimately, habits are there to keep our brain active for other things, while the habitual behaviours carry on automatically.

Just imagine if you had to analyse every potential action or behaviour before you started it. Take opening a door, for example: you must walk up to it, stretch out your right arm, open then close your hand, squeeze the handle, motion your hand clockwise whilst applying force, then, whilst moving forward, pushing the door in tandem with the pace of your movement in order to progress through the door. No one consciously follows these steps. It's because of repetition that this sequence of actions has become an automatic, helpful habit.

Please take a moment to notice all the positive habits that get you through the day. They are the occasions when you act before you think and they usually have a productive outcome. These habits become entrenched in routine, as well as occurring alongside certain associations.

Of course, not all habits are great – particularly when anxiety becomes embedded as a habit within our daily lives. Unfortunately, it is extremely common for people with anxiety to constantly think about how they feel or ruminate on how anxiety may affect them in the present or at future events. To many people, the act of thinking about their anxiety, as well as resorting to general worry after a certain event, becomes a negative habit. This behaviour pattern is the result of frequent repetition.

It is important to recognise that excessive anxiety derives from an amalgamation of negative habits. However, through our behaviour we can change these habits. Before we start doing this, we must firstly understand *why* changing habits can be so effective in overcoming anxiety.

Habits with associations

A habit is a behaviour that we default to because of *repetition*.
Habits can be positive for our daily lives, but they can also
become a hindrance when the habit of focusing on anxiety
surfaces as one of them. I'd like us now to focus on the *events* that
trigger our habits, as this is incredibly important when it comes
to changing the negative habits surrounding anxiety. Whatever
the events that seem to trigger our anxiety, there are almost
always *associations* that come with these. For example, a lot of my
clients seem to become fearful of public places like supermarkets.
Therefore, any associations with supermarkets become negative,
whereupon even thinking about visiting a supermarket becomes
a trigger for a release of adrenaline. It could be argued that it is
the *negative association* with the supermarket that is responsible for
any current feelings of anxiety.

We must start to look at the associations that are linked
to our habits. Here is a list of common habits linked with
associations that I have heard at my practice:

- 'When I wake up and look up at the bedroom ceiling, I
  think, "How do I feel today?"'

- 'I don't feel "normal". Is there something wrong with me?'

- 'I'm walking into work. What will people think of me
  today?'

- 'This is a new bodily sensation. Does this mean
  something is wrong with me?'

- 'I have an upcoming social event. How will I cope?'

Much like the supermarket description, these examples
highlight negative associations with certain events. In the first
example, the person's bedroom is associated with anxiety and

focusing on how they feel, which is similar to the example of the person walking to work. These examples also highlight that 'events' can happen internally, such as the associations we possess with new bodily sensations, or not feeling quite right.

I have found that anxiety can often be triggered by the subjective associations we have with elements of our personal life. Although this can be troublesome, it doesn't mean that we can't change our *initial reaction* to these associations. It is the initial reaction that can often trigger the chain of thoughts that leave us feeling anxious. I would advise you to take time to reflect on certain times when you feel anxious and if this anxiety is part of an observable pattern. To explain this in more depth, we need to learn about neuropathways within our brains.

Neuropathways explained

Our brains all contain a multitude of neuropathways; these are like little roads that connect many areas of our brain together.

I like to picture our brains as a road map – a bit like the old school fold-out atlases we used before the days of satellite navigation, where the roads represent our neuropathways and the land mass represents the 'flesh' of our brains. For us to function, millions of electrochemical signals are sent down these little roads to make us think, move, feel emotions and exist autonomically.

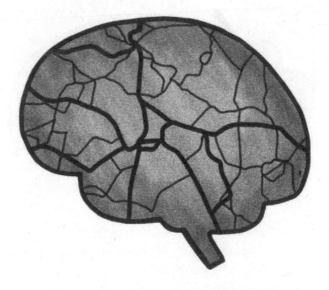

It is important to know that these electrochemical signals are required for every thought we have. For example, if I asked you to think of a pink elephant on rollerblades, then your brain would process countless signals that are sent down these little roads (neuropathways) to the required part of your brain so it can help you conjure this bizarre picture in your imagination.

To best explain how neuropathways work, I will draw upon an analogy that I use in my practice:

Picture yourself at the side of a field filled with tall grass. At the other end of the field is your *destination*. Now, to reach your destination, you can, well, walk across the field of tall grass! You might not be comfortable, but you can stamp down the grass until you eventually get to your destination. Now, let's say you have ventured to the end of the field and have reached your destination. You can look back and observe the route you have taken across the field. Naturally, you would see the path you took across the field by the tall grass being flattened where you placed your feet. Basically, you could look back and trace your steps because you have trampled the grass in order to reach your destination for the first time.

Now let's say you returned to the field a week later – back to where you first started. It is likely that the grass you trod upon has righted itself, or grown back, so if you wanted to reach your destination, you would have to venture out across the field again with little guidance. It is at this point that you realise that a simple pathway across the field would be so much easier to help you reach your destination.

Now here's the important bit: what would happen if we continued to walk over the field, in the same direction, over and over again? Well, we would flatten the grass to the point where we would make a more lasting pathway. Walking over the same space multiple times would give a more lasting effect. We could return in several weeks' time and still observe where we had trodden previously, allowing us to reach our destination with little effort. Simply put, this is how our brain develops and uses habits.

Every catchy song that you can't get out of your head, the alphabet, times tables, movie quotes and default phrases are a result of a solidified neuropathway. Every time you repeat something, it is like walking over that grass field using the same route. This is also the case for the helpful habits I mentioned previously. You can drive a car, open doors, brush your teeth and fall into an array of helpful habits because of these solid, ingrained neuropathways put in place by your use of repetition.

Strong neuropathways are what our habits use to operate and they can be really helpful. However, when our *anxious* behaviours are repeated, they too can quickly solidify and, ultimately, become a habit. We can often fall into the trap of venturing across the grass via the wrong route – ending up in the boggy swamp where we can become stuck. This is usually the part of the brain that makes us feel anxiety (the *amygdala*).

The more that we repeat anxious behaviours, the easier the route to the swamp becomes, thus making it more tempting to venture down when faced with a similar situation. It is important to understand that feelings of anxiety can occur as the result of habit, deriving from a solidified neuropathway produced by repeated behaviour.

If we look back at the example of the person who wakes up, looks up at her bedroom ceiling, then starts to focus on how she feels, then we could say that this is a habit deriving from repetition. The person has built a strong association between looking at the ceiling and how she feels internally. Therefore, using the analogy, when she wakes up, she is standing at one side of the field. She needs to cross the field and decides it is much easier to take the path most trodden. In this case, it is looking at the ceiling and focusing on how she feels. It is this path, however, that leads to the boggy swamp of anxiety. How many times have you stopped in your day just to ruminate on how you feel?

This is where habit and *associations* play a part in all of this. To change an anxious habit, we must change our associations. We can do this by choosing to create a *new* pathway across the field, as described in the analogy above, when faced with a situation that may trigger our anxiety. It requires trampling down the tall grass, at the cost of more effort, but in the long run it can benefit us massively because we can create a new, easier pathway. Ultimately, we can rewire our brains; we can do this by changing our reactions, or behaviours, in a given situation. Then, by a process of repetition, we can form new pathways which, over time, can help us form new, healthy habits.

For example, if you find that you become anxious when you have nothing to do or too much time to dwell, then the association you have with this event is to stroll down the easy path of focusing on your anxiety. Many of my clients tell me that their anxiety seems more prominent when they try to sit still or lie down. Now what usually happens here is that when we sit down, our default habit is to dwell on how we feel. We do this because it's easy, as there exists a strong neuropathway formed through repetition. We have strolled along the same path across the field so many times that it has become a habit.

To change this habit, we must consciously change our
behaviour when this occurs. This can apply to any scenario
where you notice yourself getting anxious. Here's the simple
bit: by literally doing anything *but* dwelling on the anxiety,
we already avoid going all the way down the old path and we
begin to form a new one. Focusing on or doing anything else,
apart from dwelling on how we feel, helps us to start forming
a new neuropathway in our brain. Then, the more we copy
this behaviour, the stronger this new neuropathway becomes,
and the weaker the old one.

I'm not going to tell you what works for you, as this is up
to you to decide. What you will notice is that, through the
repetition of a new behaviour, you will start to instil a new
habit that will replace the old one. Some examples from
previous clients include: the use of a Rubik's cube, reading
a book, calling a friend, washing the dishes, exercising or
meditation – to name a few.

Now you might be thinking, *'So every time I get anxious I
have to resort to an odd behaviour. What use is that?'* Well, we
initially change the anxious behaviour so we can *weaken*
the old neuropathway; then, as time progresses, we can
give ourselves more thought options when we are faced
with an event that can trigger our anxiety. Over time, we
can add in new habits, so it becomes less and less tempting
to follow old pathways, or old habits. Old neuropathways
can and will weaken – just think of someone who has
given up smoking.

To remind yourself of how powerful a habit can be,
imagine your friend enthusiastically singing the first line
of the chorus of your favourite song. They turn to you;
what do you do? Well, you'd probably let those solidified
neuropathways decide.

Just remember that excessive anxiety is not helped – and is often perpetuated – by negative thought habits. Change the bad habits by changing your behaviour.

Self-reassurance and the TA Diagram

After studying feedback from my previous book, I have concluded that one of its main strengths is its ability to provide *reassurance* for those who are highly anxious. It was the *reassurance* that brought anxiety levels down, not the fact that the book could magically transform our sympathetic nervous system and our adrenal glands. The concept of reassurance – more importantly self-reassurance – is integral to managing and overcoming excessive anxiety. Ultimately, the first book told us that we're *going to be okay*, despite how anxious we may feel. The aim was to try to establish a *core belief* that what we were feeling was 'just anxiety' and that it would eventually pass. Furthermore, the book placed emphasis on not fearing anxiety or perceiving it as something that's dangerous.

If we can teach ourselves the skill of self-reassurance, particularly at times when we feel anxious, then we can actively lower our anxiety on our own and without the need for external assurances. When inspected through the (metaphorical) magnifying glass, the skill of self-reassurance is, in a nutshell, the way in which we speak to ourselves. It is the ability to observe how we speak to ourselves when anxious, and then change the tone to something more appropriate. Furthermore, and perhaps most importantly, in a lot of cases it is the way we speak to ourselves that actually *causes* the anxiety. However, for this section, I will focus on the times when we are anxious.

To help me explain this further, I have borrowed the *Parent, Adult and Child* (PAC) diagram from the Transactional Analysis

(TA) school of thought. I have moulded it to help me best explain how we can 'speak', or interact, with ourselves when we are anxious. It is important to note that TA is a form of therapy that practitioners can study for years; the modified diagram used in this section is merely a representation of my own rudimentary understanding of the model.

According to TA, everyone has three modes of personality: a *parent* mode, an *adult* mode and a *child* mode. We all, at some point, access these modes, either by default or as a reaction to a situation or interaction with another person. None of the modes are necessarily 'bad', but sometimes they are not appropriate for a given situation:

CHILD MODE

Not to be confused with 'childish', child mode encapsulates the emotions we experience that are more commonly associated with children. Child mode has two sides to it, the first being 'playful child' and the other 'needing child'.

Playful child is the part of our personality where we like to have fun — usually laughing, jesting, revelling in food fights, thriving creatively and utilising a lot of the imagination. If you observe a group of adults or children all laughing and playing, then I feel this personifies playful child mode the most appropriately. Playful child is the most fun of the modes of personality.

Needing child mode is the part of our personality where we feel we need reassurance on some level. A classic example is the scenario of a toddler falling over and grazing his knee. He looks up to his parent for reassurance, perhaps because he's never seen blood before, and the parent then comforts and reassures the toddler. Needing child mode is when we find ourselves upset or angry, with our emotions dictating our behaviours. Needing child can also see us seeking reassurance from others.

ADULT MODE

Adult mode is the mode of personality reserved for pragmatism, logic and problem-solving. I like to think of adult mode as a way of communicating with others in a reasoned and mature way, a bit like people in a business meeting, or someone planning an important event. Adult mode instructs our behaviours to act out of logic, rather than impulsively through our emotions. If you have ever successfully managed to resolve a disagreement with someone, then the likelihood is that both of you achieved this in adult mode.

PARENT MODE

Like child mode, parent mode has two sides to it: these are *nurturing* parent mode and something I like to call *disciplinary* or *lecturing* parent mode.

Nurturing parent mode is when we offer compassion and empathy, as well as providing reassurance to others. For example, if we have an upset friend, we may access nurturing parent mode by giving our friend a hug, or reassuring them that things will be OK. The parent in the toddler scenario may also do the same, perhaps by cuddling the toddler and letting them know that the graze is nothing to be afraid of. Nurturing parent mode quite often provides reassurance that transcends logic and reason, where the act of being kind and empathetic is enough to make someone feel better.

Disciplinary parent is the mode that is characterised by the need to lecture, criticise and, often, become negatively authoritative. If you've ever been 'lectured' by someone, told off, or informed that you haven't met expectations, the other person will have been behaving in disciplinary parent mode. If you have ever witnessed a heated argument, or debate, it is usually the result of the participants thinking that they each 'know better' – another strong trait of this type of parent mode.

A good way to familiarise yourself with the modes of personality is to analyse how you interact with others in your relationships. For example, my best friend and I often spend a lot of time in playful child mode – a mode that's reciprocated and it works positively. Another example is the interaction with an old boss of mine. I would try to communicate with her in adult mode, but was often met with lecturing and criticism stemming from disciplinary parent which, in turn, triggered my own transition into needing child mode because it made me feel upset.

Below are some examples of how people's modes of personality can interact:

PERSON 1 PERSON 2

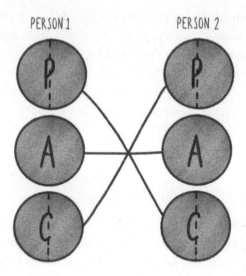

Adult to adult: Two adults planning an event, solving a problem, talking formally, being respectful, analysing a situation or talking politely despite negative feelings. This could be between any two adults, such as a work meeting, a teenage son and his parent, a married couple, two friends out for lunch or dealing with a telemarketing call.

Child to parent: A child falls over and grazes her knee. She looks up to her parent for reassurance. Parent, in *nurturing parent* mode, hugs the child, puts a plaster on and tells the child that she will be alright. Child feels reassured and content. No explanation required.

In a similar scenario, the child falls over and looks for reassurance from her parent. However, the parent is in *disciplinary parent* mode and chooses to reprimand the child for being clumsy. The parent then lectures the child on how to be careful when walking, focusing on what the child 'should' have done.

Child to child: Two adults in *needing child* mode are arguing about whose problems are more important. Both adults are upset and in need of reassurance. This leads to squabbling, shouting and crying. Neither of the adults in this scenario could access *parent* mode to reassure the other. Similarly, this could be two children arguing in a schoolyard.

Two adults in *playful child* mode are laughing, play-fighting and mocking each other. They could be out for a drink, singing songs in the car, or playing a sport together. Everything is playful and good-natured.

Parent to Parent: Two adults in *lecturing parent* mode are arguing about who is right about a certain topic. Both feel that they are superior to the other person. Their points are motivated by a desire to be perceived as more knowledgeable. This can cause sustained conflict.

Two adults in *nurturing parent* mode are reassuring each other that they are OK. This could be comforting each other in a relationship or reaffirming a strong friendship.

Adult to Child: This scenario includes two adults, where one is trying to remain reasonable whilst the other remains in *needing child* mode. For example, a paramedic could be interacting with a drunk person who is upset and she is trying to explain that it's in the person's best interests to be taken to hospital.

A classic example is when an adult, or child, seeks emotional reassurance from an adult, but is greeted with a logical or pragmatic response, rather than the emotional *parent* that was being sought after. For example, a teenage boy could approach his father upset about a relationship and his father, in *adult* mode, could explain the logistics of the situation and the next step, rather than providing an emotional response.

Another example is when an adult in *playful child* mode tries to fool around with another adult in *adult* mode, but the other adult is busy doing work, so suggests that they put off being silly for another time.

Modes of personality and anxiety

When it comes to dealing with anxiety, people often operate in a mode of personality that is detrimental to alleviating their negative feelings. In my experience, I have found that people often respond to their anxiety in the mode of *needing child, lecturing parent* and attempts at *adult* mode.

In *needing child* mode, we look to others to help us feel better, for example not wanting to be left alone, or asking others to make us feel better. *Lecturing parent* is used when we become frustrated – we often criticise ourselves for being anxious by not accepting it or comparing ourselves to an idealised social norm. Furthermore, attempts to try to solve the problem 'rationally', or by simply using a logical approach, often aren't effective. I attribute this to the fact that the complexity of strong emotions can't be understood by using observational logic alone.

The aim of this section is to help you understand that the most appropriate mode of personality to address anxiety is *nurturing parent*. This mode of personality is the part of us that can provide reassurance to others, and also to ourselves. In my experience of practice, I have found that a common factor linking a lot of people who experience anxiety disorders is an inability to speak to oneself in nurturing parent mode. We often criticise ourselves in lecturing parent mode for not meeting the standards we have set for ourselves, but when it comes to experiencing the frightening feelings associated with anxiety, nurturing parent mode is absolutely essential.

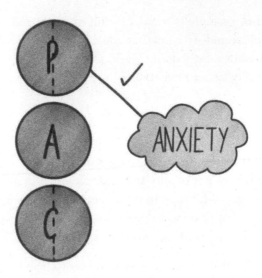

I recommend taking some time out to analyse how you talk to yourself in different situations. If you notice that you address your anxiety by criticising yourself and becoming frustrated (*lecturing parent*), running away or seeking reassurance from others (*needing child*), or by approaching the issue from a solely logical point of view (*adult* mode), then try to see how you can approach your anxiety using a self-nurturing approach.

The Thought Pie Chart

On average, it is believed that we experience around 60,000 thoughts a day. Visualizing a summary of these thoughts is something that both my clients and I feel is very helpful in shaping our perspective. Firstly, I'd like you, from a hypothetical perspective, to organise your daily thoughts into three groups: thoughts about the *past*, thoughts in the *present* and thoughts about the *future*. Then, using a pie chart diagram, try to apportion a segment for each group, to give a simple picture of how they measure up.

I've taken an example of a client who suffers with health anxiety below:

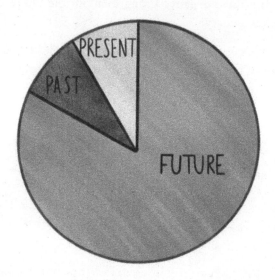

As you can see, the largest segment of the pie chart is given over to *future* thoughts. Thoughts about the future can be perfectly normal. For example, planning a day ahead, future events, family planning, career options, holidays and car journeys are future thoughts necessary for everyday life. However, when these future thoughts become entwined with anxiety, they are often dictated by the *Three Core Statements of Anxiety*, mentioned previously.

In this particular case, the client is often worrying about the immediate future regarding their health. Here are some examples of their thoughts:

- 'What if there's something wrong with my stomach?'
- 'I can't go to the doctor; I am too scared.'
- 'I should seek reassurance and change my eating habits.'
- 'What if I leave it and it gets worse?'

So, in summary, a person with health anxiety may be prone to thoughts revolving around the future rather than in the present. It is these negative thoughts about the future which fuel further anxiety.

Here is an example of someone fearing a panic attack, or in the midst of panic disorder (such as myself at one time):

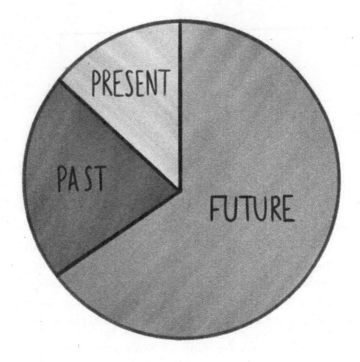

The person in this example is also spending a lot of time thinking about the future. Some examples may include:

- 'What if I'm about to have a panic attack?'
- 'What if I panic in public?'
- 'What if I freak out at work?'

- 'I can't cope outside.'
- 'I should wait until I feel better.'

There is also a significant portion of thoughts dedicated to the *past*. This may include ruminating on the possible reasons why they feel anxious or trying to 'work out' their current feelings.

Here is an example of a client with social anxiety:

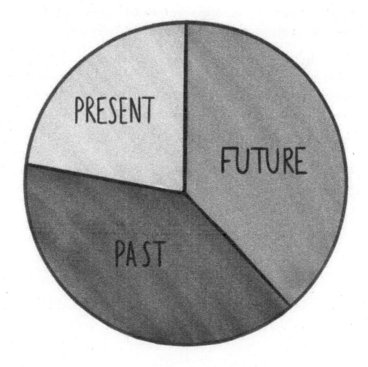

Social anxiety can often include worrying about how we are perceived by others, predominantly in the past and the future. For example, we could worry about what we said to someone, for instance a bold joke, or if we have caused offence. Similarly, we could worry about an upcoming social event where we doubt our ability to cope in the situation.

The point I'm trying to make in this section is that we seem to feel at our best when our thoughts are in the *present*. A lot of my clients state that they feel less anxious when they are occupied, like when they are at work or absorbed in an activity, for example. Furthermore, childhood – for many people – is often a time where we felt less anxious compared to how we feel in the present. A lot of emphasis on play and indulging in new experiences seems to take priority, rather than the plethora of worries that adulthood seems to conjure.

I believe that to access a less anxious mindset, we must try our best to let our mind be in the *present*. A lot of anxious people unknowingly try to access this mindset when they try to 'distract' themselves from how they feel: by doing chores, completing puzzles or playing with their smart devices, for example. How to knowingly access the present, however, is different for each individual. Personally, I feel meditation is an excellent way to access 'present' thinking, but it isn't necessarily for everyone. This will be discussed further in Part 5.

Summary and Step Four

I feel that the ultimate aim of the anxious person is to start building up a strong *core belief* that they're actually 'OK'. Remember that anxiety cannot actually hurt you, it's just very unpleasant. When we start panicking about our anxiety, it means that we've been abiding by a temporary belief that has disappeared as soon as the anxious response has kicked in.

A good way to start building a strong core belief is to challenge yourself in situations where you become anxious, regardless of where you are. This could be a situation where anxiety has come on suddenly, or somewhere that you habitually avoid because you're afraid of how it will make you feel. The *associations* you have with the feeling of rising anxiety, or the situation you are in, will undoubtedly be strong, but remember that you can change these through your behaviours. By going against the impulse to run away, or avoid, we automatically start changing the negative association with the event by changing the habit (neuropathway) connected with the event.

For example, I have worked with many clients who have been afraid of getting on the London Underground rail network. They have perhaps used it many times in the past but, because of anxiety, they have developed a negative association with it. Their fears revolve around: not being able to cope on the train; fearing a panic attack on the train; fear of passing out; and the fear of embarrassing themselves. Ultimately, these people did not have a core belief that they would be OK.

To change this association, the clients began to change their behaviours surrounding the fear. Firstly, they would go to the tube station, feel the anxiety, measure it on their scale, then continue to go *against* what their anxious mind would say to them, e.g. *'What if you have an anxiety attack here?'* You could say that they were 'pretending' they weren't anxious; they were forming new neuropathways and ignoring the older, easier ones. This is difficult to begin with, but it gets easier with practice. Some of my clients broke it down into manageable chunks, such as staying on the tube for one stop, or just spending time on the platform and waiting for the anxiety to settle.

By repeating the behaviour of going to the Underground and challenging these feelings, the clients began changing their associations by creating new neuropathways, which ultimately led to establishing a core belief that they were OK. Sometimes this can work very quickly, but more often than not it takes a lot of repetition. If you are someone who has ever overcome a fear or phobia, you'll know how the brain can quickly establish something as 'safe'.

Start to lay the foundations for establishing a core belief by changing habits and associations. It requires resilience and hard work, but the rewards are priceless.

PART 5

Lifestyle Choices

It somewhat irks me to see that a lot of the professional advice associated with treating anxiety is predominantly reactionary or grounded in the belief that an immediate change in one's life, on a fairly superficial level, can alleviate the symptoms of anxiety. Issues like diet, exercise and medication all have their place, of course, but I fear that focusing primarily on these, rather than the deeper 'layers' of beliefs and behaviours, can run the risk of an anxious person expending all their energy away from what is most beneficial.

You can see how a heavy focus on lifestyle changes can actually have a negative effect by referring back to the 'If I ...' plant: if we put our faith in eradicating certain foods, taking supplements, running a marathon or practising elements of 'pseudo-science' as a solution to alleviating excessive anxiety, then we can actually cause ourselves *increased* levels of worry if these actions don't have the desired effect. Furthermore, if they do have a positive effect (which they can), we also run the risk of establishing a belief that we cannot function without them. For example, a man may feel that if he doesn't exercise every day, then he'll become anxious. He may also feel that if he eats gluten, or certain specific foods, he will also become anxious.

This chapter looks at the benefits that certain lifestyle choices can produce but, at the same time, stresses the importance of maintaining a realistic perspective on them. This chapter is written from my experience as a psychotherapist as well as from my personal life.

Meditation

When working in my practice, I have often found that people seem to shudder whenever the topic of meditation is brought up. Furthermore, I often hear of experiences where people have 'tried' meditation, but to no avail. If I'm being honest, I initially approached the idea with a similar attitude; I liked to regard myself as someone who is 'logical' and dismissed meditation as something 'spiritual' and alien to me.

Along with many 'experts' in the field, however, I have since discovered that meditation can be highly beneficial, particularly for those who have anxiety averaging at about a 3 to 6 on the Anxiety Scale. On the other hand, reflecting on my own experience, I wouldn't necessarily recommend it for the highly anxious – not until the person feels sufficiently informed and comfortable with their situation. For the highly anxious, meditation can often put you in a position where you are forced to 'stop' and, as a result, made to feel extremely uncomfortable.

There are various definitions and interpretations of meditation. Personally, I prefer to abide by and promote the *mindfulness* model, as I feel it represents a stripped-back and modernised version of the ancient practice. I can also explain it to people with reference to our habits and the neuropathways I was explaining before.

Firstly, meditation can help us *observe* our thoughts. To some people, this is quite a strange concept. Observing a thought requires us to take a step back and somehow *watch* ourselves thinking. This is a skill that can be practised over time and is incredibly helpful as it enables us to realise that a thought is … well, *just a thought*. Nothing more. I can *think* that the world is going to end in five minutes, but the reality is that it will not.

As you'll probably be aware, it can be quite difficult to dismiss anxious thoughts as 'just a thought', particularly when we become absorbed by them and the '*What if*'s feel like a legitimate danger. However, when we practise observing our thoughts, through meditation, it can become easier to distinguish a scary thought as being a case of 'just anxiety' rather than anything anchored in reality. Learning to observe a thought can help us to distance ourselves from it, rather than immediately believing everything that the imagination conjures.

Secondly, practising meditation can go a long way in terms of changing our anxious habits. It helps to train us to stop dwelling on certain anxious thoughts, as well as bringing us into the *present* – something we saw the importance of in the Thought Pie Chart section. Let me use a simplified example, with reference to the neuropathways analogy from before, to explain how this works.

Let's say that a particular thought makes us feel anxious and obsessed. For example, planning to go to a social event when we have social anxiety (or focusing on a physical symptom and obsessing about it). The mere thought of the event or the symptom can trigger anxiety, so we may spend days at home obsessing and negatively speculating about something that might happen, rather than siding with the reality of the situation. As we know, it is easy to fall into a habit when we react to an anxious thought, as the neuropathways associated with the event have been used plenty of times – the easy path across the field of tall grass (see Part 4).

Meditation can be an excellent skill to turn to, as it can snap us out of the habit of dwelling, or ruminating, by focusing our attention elsewhere. In a lot of meditative practice, this is usually when we are guided to focus on the *breath*. Simply put, I feel meditation works for anxiety because, logically, any time spent focusing on the breath is less time focusing on the anxious thoughts. Furthermore, the less time spent focusing on anxious thoughts, the less the body reacts to the thoughts, thus leading to fewer hormones being released via the fight-or-flight response, and so on.

That's not to say, however, that the anxious thoughts disappear altogether when we attempt to focus on the breath. This is not the aim. Referring to the neuropathway / field of tall grass analogy, just by *attempting* to steer our focus away from the anxious thoughts (to the breath) is enough to start forming a new neuropathway, or 'route' across the field. Ultimately, the more we attempt to focus on anything besides the anxious thought or feeling, the stronger the new neuropathways can become – and the *weaker* the old, negative one.

When beginning to practise meditation, keep in mind that the only aim is to steer your focus back to something in the moment. The aim is not to block out anxious thoughts, but to notice any thoughts and then to choose to focus our attention elsewhere – on the breath, for example. Try not to fall into the trap of becoming frustrated with yourself if you keep referring back to the anxiety. Instead, praise yourself when you catch yourself focusing elsewhere, then bring yourself back into the moment.

There are plenty of meditation guides available through books, the internet, workshops and classes. Personally, I still use a couple of mobile apps that guide you through the process. I always advocate it as a way of spending more time in the present, as well as rewiring those neuropathways that make focusing on anxiety such a dominant part of our lives.

Exercise

Now I wouldn't be suggesting anything revolutionary by stating that exercise can be a good way to alleviate anxiety. After all, if we have built up adrenaline and cortisol flowing through our veins, then exercise can be a good way to expel the excess bodily chemicals and trigger our parasympathetic nervous system. It is often suggested, through many platforms, that exercise can go some way in helping the anxiety sufferer. However, we should consider how we can incorporate exercise in a healthy way, rather than simply relying on it as a form of escapism.

Firstly, we must look at what motivates us to exercise. If it's simply to rid ourselves of anxiety, then we may make the mistake of relying on it too much to function. Referring to the '*If I ...*' plant from Part 2, we may falsely believe that if we exercise, then we can rid ourselves of our anxiety. This, however, leaves us vulnerable if we are ever incapacitated for any reason – an injury, for example. If we solely rely on exercise as the antidote for our excessive anxiety, then we run the risk of having no coping strategy when facing some of life's events. The '*If I ...*' plant is relevant here because sometimes we can focus all our energy on the routine of exercise, rather than dealing with the root of the problem.

Furthermore, if we are a particularly anxious person, who lives each day with a high average on the *Anxiety Scale*, then we may be in the situation where our body is crying out for *rest*. The anxious and stressed person will often be 'running on adrenaline', where the body has not had enough time to recover, nor does it have the resources to draw upon to carry out a normal daily routine. Adding a long run or an intense gym session on top of that can run the risk of exhaustion.

What I always recommend to my clients is to treat exercise more as an accompaniment to recovery. It is also highly beneficial if you can turn that exercise into something fun, rather than seeing it as a chore. For example, back when I was very anxious, I used to play indoor football with friends, or go for scenic walks, rather than abiding by a mindset where I felt I needed to exercise. If I found myself too tired, then I would simply choose to rest.

All in all, I advocate the use of exercise to promote your overall well-being; it can be particularly useful if you are also dealing with depression. However, I would also suggest that you shouldn't 'overdo it'. When it comes to choosing *which* form of exercise to try, this is simply up to you. I have seen many clients who report that activities such as yoga, walking, Tai Chi, sports and swimming have been a great accompaniment to overcoming their anxiety.

Rest

Rest and relaxation are so important when it comes to recovery. In fact, I would go so far as to say that a person's inability to do just this is a large contributor to developing an anxiety condition. When I work with clients who have been diagnosed with Generalised Anxiety Disorder (GAD), I often give them a scenario to imagine and they speculate how they might deal with it. I suggest you have a try:

Imagine you are in an empty room with only a chair to sit on. You have no phone, nothing in particular to focus on and only your thoughts to sit with. How do you think you would feel?

The responses often fall along the lines of '*I don't think I could cope!*', or '*That sounds like a nightmare!*'. This scenario tends to reveal more about the person, as it suggests that the action of stopping and being alone with their thoughts is something that they are not comfortable with. It also tells me that, when it comes to lifestyle, the person probably rests very little. Therefore, their parasympathetic nervous system hardly ever has the chance to kick in and revive them.

In Part 3, when discussing the *Three Core Statements of Anxiety*, I mentioned the second statement: the *'I should ...'*. I have found, both with my clients and in my own experience, that this statement often acts as a barrier to much-needed rest. Ironically, the *'I should ...'* often seems to promote various tasks from our mental 'to-do' lists, whilst dismissing arguably the most important task: rest and recuperation. Unfortunately, effective resting seems to be a skill that a lot of anxious people have either never learned or forgotten about, as it can so easily fall down the list of priorities in hectic adult life.

When we find ourselves anxious and 'on edge', we can take this as a sign that the sympathetic nervous system has been hogging all the attention. The goal of rest and recuperation is to bring about more balance within the body by activating the *parasympathetic* nervous system. However, this is easier said than done.

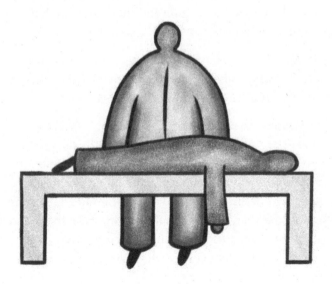

It is important to highlight that the concept of rest is subjective to the individual; every person will have their own preferences when it comes to resting or 'switching off'. I wish I could lay out a set of instructions for you, at the end of which you find yourself resting thanks to an easy step-by-step guide. Effective resting, however, is something you will have to work out for yourself. Personally, I like to play a video game, watch TV or read a book. I also like to get myself a massage now and then as a treat. This helps me to switch off and recover from a stressful day. Importantly, I *allow* myself to do this and dismiss any thoughts revolving around an urge to do something 'more productive'; resting is the most productive thing I can do when it is needed.

Learning to rest is a matter of changing your internal dialogue – something I'll discuss next.

Positive self-dialogue

In the self-reassurance section of Part 4, we discussed how important it is to be kind to yourself when anxious. It is too often the case that we can grow frustrated and angry with ourselves for being fearful or worried, especially when we've lived with the feelings for a long time. In the instance of a panic attack, the use of kind self-reassurance can go a long way in helping to bring our anxiety down from those 9s and 10s on the Anxiety Scale. In our daily lives, however, I would like to stress the importance of maintaining a positive self-dialogue, even when we feel it isn't needed.

This positive self-dialogue works wonders when, firstly, we find ourselves in stressful times and, secondly, when we actually mean it. If we replace the habit of self-criticising when things don't go our way with an emphasis on giving ourselves a pat on the back now and then, we can offset anxiety before it begins to build and, instead, facilitate a lifestyle where we are constantly self-nurturing.

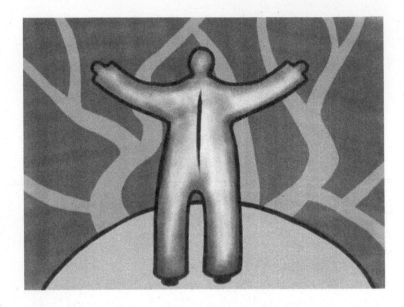

As a psychotherapist, I have discovered that this is particularly difficult for those who have never really learned that giving praise is OK, never mind self-praise. Praising and reassuring ourselves that we're doing a 'good job' with life can be particularly difficult if we haven't been raised in an environment where this behaviour was prevalent. The ability to be kind to ourselves can be severely lacking if we were neglected or harshly criticised by others when growing up. Sometimes we have to fill in the blanks that we perhaps did not learn during childhood. That's not to say that our parents did a bad job – nobody is perfect!

I advocate giving yourself some praise – either in your mind or aloud – at any time of day and as many times as you want. Give yourself a 'well done' if you complete a task such as washing the dishes. Remind yourself that it's OK if you failed to get something done by a certain time. If you make a mistake, then try to go with the flow and see it as a learning opportunity.

By learning to 'speak' to yourself in a kind manner, you can prevent the gradual build-up of stress that triggers our sympathetic nervous system and, in contrast, go as far as to stimulate the kinder parasympathetic nervous system – the part of our nervous system responsible for helping us to feel good. Furthermore, continuous self-praise can help us to formulate a helpful new *habit*. We can form new, healthier neuropathways and the associations we have with our day-to-day behaviours can change for the better.

Please don't underestimate how powerful self-praise can be and its role in lessening and overcoming anxiety. It can often cause a 'cringe' reaction in people – particularly in British culture, where modesty and humility are somewhat revered. It takes practice and can be difficult to begin with but, as when forming any habit, with time and repetition it starts to feel natural to us.

Counselling

Counselling and talking therapy can be hugely beneficial both in terms of alleviating anxiety and discovering more about ourselves. Unfortunately, the topic of counselling remains a societal taboo. I can still recall my own reluctance to seek counselling during my time tussling with anxiety and depression. I suppose I feared there would be consequences if anyone 'found out' about it, especially as I once saw it as important that people saw me as an 'ideal' configuration of self; I didn't want to be perceived as 'weak' or incompetent, so I avoided communicating what I was feeling and experiencing. In reality, counselling remains a practice built upon the foundation of *confidentiality*, so making the decision to talk to a professional does not need to be explicitly advertised.

Similar to my views on meditation, I believe that counselling can be a great accompaniment to anxiety recovery, although not necessarily essential. After all, why would you buy a book on anxiety only to be told to seek counselling? I have included this section to inform people of the options available, as I feel that access to counselling services is somewhat hindered by a lack of information available to the public.

As a psychotherapist, it is essential that I myself attend frequent counselling sessions – both to look after myself and also provide the fairest and best possible service to my clients. However, given my positive experience of the counselling process, I can safely say that it is something I would incorporate into my life regardless of my chosen career path. Having someone to talk to, who lies outside the boundaries of your own life and remains neutral and unbiased, can be a powerful cathartic tool – particularly if you are in an emotionally demanding stage of your life.

There are many different types of counselling, which is something I believe can be confusing to someone who may be considering seeking professional help and advice. Therefore, I have provided a brief overview of some of the options available:

COGNITIVE BEHAVIOURAL THERAPY (CBT)

If you have ever sought help from your doctor for anxiety, the likelihood is that you would have been referred for CBT and also offered the option of taking medication. CBT is a psycho-social intervention therapy that is built upon an educative approach to dealing with thoughts, feelings and emotions.

CBT aims to look at how we think and how this, in turn, affects our behaviours. Personally, I find some of the educative

elements of CBT to be very helpful, as well as the use of
quantifying feelings using a scale. It can be encouraging to see
your 'improvement' on paper and the results of reflecting and
changing certain thought habits. CBT is very directive and
includes quite a bit of 'homework' and requires you to invest
your time in reflecting outside the sessions.

PERSON-CENTRED THERAPY (PCT)

In contrast to CBT, person-centred counselling is a very
non-directive form of talking therapy. Have you ever wished
that you could just have a room that was separate from the
world, where you could rant and rave about your worries and
concerns? In PCT, the counsellor encourages you to lead the
sessions and allows you to bring any topic of conversation
that you'd like to the table. The role of the counsellor is to
listen and reflect back to you what they have heard – offering
a fresh perspective using only the information that you
communicate.

PCT can be helpful in many ways and can often empower
the person to discover things about themselves that they, at
one point, may have been to reluctant to explore. The person-
centred counsellor is non-diagnostic, so don't worry about
having your feelings judged and pitched against existing
psychological theory.

TRANSACTIONAL ANALYSIS (TA)

I have borrowed and adapted a loose theory from TA in the
section entitled Self-Assurance: The TA Diagram. TA therapy
looks at the 'interactions' that we have in our lives and explores
the three 'ego states' in which we can find ourselves behaving,
these ego states being labelled *Parent, Adult* and *Child*. For more

information, you can visit www.ericberne.com to see an easily accessible overview of this therapeutic approach.

PSYCHODYNAMIC THERAPY

The Psychodynamic approach to therapy aims to bring the unconscious mind back into conscious awareness. It aims to help individuals work out the root of feelings, perhaps buried within the subconscious, that we may still be holding on to. Psychodynamic therapy has its origins within the works of Sigmund Freud, Carl Jung, Alfred Adler, Melanie Klein and Otto Rank.

DIALECTICAL BEHAVIOUR THERAPY (DBT)

Dialectical Behaviour Therapy is a talking treatment and is similar to CBT. DBT, however, is tailored more towards people who experience emotions on a very intense and often debilitating level. It also differs from CBT as the approach focuses more on present self-acceptance, as well as utilising the strength of relationship with the therapist.

COGNITIVE ANALYTICAL THERAPY (CAT)

Cognitive Analytical Therapy comprises two components: the first being the 'analytical' and the second the 'cognitive' side. The analytical side aims to explore previous events in the client's life that could link, or relate, to what the client is experiencing now. The cognitive focus comes after a relationship with the therapist has been established. Together, the client and the therapist look at the potential implications of the past experiences discussed, then draw upon techniques from cognitive therapy to develop new tools and coping mechanisms.

OTHER THERAPIES

There are plenty of other options available that approach therapy from different perspectives. This part of the book has provided a basic outline of some of the most common approaches. If therapy is something that interests you, then I recommend looking through your local counselling directory. Remember, you can always contact therapists to ask about their approach.

Go with your 'non-anxious' you

I'd like to think that the main message from my previous book was to persuade the reader that it is 'OK' to go with the non-anxious version of ourselves. This means trying to ignore our anxiety and trusting in a *core belief* that we're OK and that anxiety shouldn't be able to prevent us from doing what we would usually do. We don't have to feel completely like our usual selves, nor should we measure or compare ourselves against how things were when we felt 'normal'. However, given everything that we have discussed in this book, going with our non-anxious selves would seem like the most logical option.

Firstly, we need to 'test' out a core belief that we are OK. This means making the decision to do something that makes us anxious, like going to a social event, using public transport, going to work, striking up a conversation, going to the supermarket, or getting on an aeroplane – to name just a few examples. Remember, the aim isn't to compare ourselves in these situations – we know we are already anxious – but to see if anything 'bad' happens other than perhaps a rise on our *Anxiety Scales*. Often, we will be able to get through the event unscathed, which can go some way to persuading the anxious mind that it was wrong to doubt us.

Furthermore, by doing this, we are actively rerouting our neuropathways and strengthening newer, healthier ones, or at least reinvigorating old ones that we used more often when we were less anxious. This is why repeating activities that make us uncomfortable is so important. We don't have to be '100%' and feel fully engaged in what we are doing, but the mere decision to ignore anxious habits, such as avoiding events or staying inside, is enough to formulate a new neuropathway that can help us in the future. I recommend trying this for yourself. Remember to observe your anxiety scale the more you do something – you'll find that your anxiety score will lower and lower the more you repeat something that makes you feel uncomfortable.

If you find yourself avoiding something that you would previously have engaged with, then this is the opportune moment to test the belief that you will be OK. It may take a few attempts, but observe and tap into your *nurturing parent* mode and revel in the results of your bravery.

Summary and Step Five

This chapter has looked at lifestyle choices and things we can do now to move forward. I cannot emphasise enough the importance of utilising positive self-dialogue in our day-to-day lives, as well as using activities such as meditation, exercise and rest to help keep us in the present. Lifestyle choices can go a long way towards helping us to feel more positive and to lessen the burden of our anxiety. However, I would argue that they do not present a solution for completely eradicating anxiety. I believe that understanding where our anxiety has come from, through education, self-exploration and, perhaps, counselling, is essential to a full recovery.

I have done my best to provide an overview of what I understand about anxiety, both in this and my previous book – drawing on personal experiences and my work at The Panic Room, as well as knowledge gathered from my studies. However, we must understand that we are all individuals with our own subjective experiences, core beliefs, personal values and ideals. I sincerely hope that my books will help empower you to understand your own anxiety and implement the necessary changes to live a happy and healthy life.

Emergency Panic Attack Help Pages

If you currently feel that you're very anxious, or perhaps panicking at this very moment, then read on and refer to these pages if panic ever strikes again. This part of the book has been borrowed from *Anxiety: Panicking about Panic*, as it had a huge positive response. Feel free to read it to yourself, to someone else who is panicking, or to someone who may want to help you:

OK, so you're panicking…

Let me guess:

Racing thoughts?

Feelings of terror, doom and even fear of death? Feel like you're going insane?

I know it feels horrible. I've had many panic attacks myself.

You need to realise that nothing bad is going to happen to you.

Absolutely nothing.

Your thoughts at this moment in time are merely a projection of your fears.

…This is not the reality of the situation.

You will calm down eventually.

You may not know this, but there's a ton of adrenaline and cortisol flowing through your veins at this very moment.

They're harmless bodily chemicals. You're in no danger.

You have entered 'fight-or-flight' mode. You are in no danger.

None at all.

Soon the adrenaline will run out. I know this because the adrenal glands exhaust themselves.

Your body can't maintain this panic.

It's biologically impossible.

I'm going to assume that you feel like this panic has come out of nowhere and that it feels out of your control.

You are fine.

This is normal.

Do not run away.

It is just the adrenaline. You are in 'fight-or-flight' mode.

Do you feel very different?

Does everything around you feel different?

They should do, because this is normal at a time like this.

It's just the adrenaline.

Is your mind racing?

A thousand thoughts a second?

Fearing the worst of your predicament?

This is also normal at a time like this.

It's just the adrenaline.

I bet this has happened before, perhaps many a time.

I bet this panic feels just as overwhelming as the other occasions when you've panicked, despite the previous experiences that you've had.

Wherever you are and whatever you're doing, you need to realise that nothing 'bad' is going to happen.

Believe me on this one.

I know how hard it is to 'think straight' when dealing with panic.

All you need to know is that your body has released a lot of harmless adrenaline into your system. Also, your nervous system is on high alert.

You have entered 'fight-or-flight' mode.

It's just the adrenaline.

This is normal.

This 'fight-or-flight' mode causes all sorts of changes in the mind and body.

It distorts our reality, makes our heart beat fast, makes us shake, sweat and shiver.

Believe me when I say that adrenaline can cause so many temporary, harmless changes within the body.

It does not matter if you chose to enter 'fight-or-flight' mode or not. It is happening, and it will pass quickly if you acknowledge what is going on within your body.

Steady your breathing, let the adrenaline pass and let the nervous system settle.

This feeling will pass soon.

Look forward to the fact that when the adrenal gland exhausts itself, it brings a feeling of light euphoria to the mind and body.

Look forward to this – it is a truly amazing feeling.

Keep doing what you were supposed to be doing, whether you're at home, at work, travelling or even on holiday.

The feeling will eventually pass.

Do not show this feeling the attention that it does not deserve. Continue with your day and, if the feeling ever strikes again, it will not be as intense as this time – I guarantee.

Keep active and focus on something positive. This is hard, but even thinking about something positive diverts the negative thoughts your mind is homing in on.

Everything will be fine. Nothing bad is going to happen.

Nothing bad can happen.

You can do it.

It's just the adrenaline.

Practical About Panic: An Overview

This final section provides a brief overview, or summary, of what we have covered in this book. I have broken it down into the 'Steps' provided in the summaries.

Step One

Part 1 of the book places emphasis on understanding what anxiety is, both as a feeling and from a physiological perspective. I talk about the 'fight-or-flight' response – particularly the role of hormones, such as adrenaline, and the nervous system and the effects these can have on the body. Raising our awareness of this and reassuring ourselves that feelings of fear have a physiological cause – that you can change – is where I believe every person should start when beginning to tackle excessive anxiety.

Step Two

Part 2 looked at putting our anxiety into perspective. Firstly, we looked at some of the common habits of the anxious, such as chasing a miracle thought, catastrophising, avoidance, escapism, abiding by the '*If I* ...' plant, controlling our environment and placing anxiety at the centre of our lives.

We then looked at attempting to simplify our own anxiety, through the use of the Anxiety Umbrella, rather than exhausting our resources on each individual '*What if* ...', worry or concern. Then we explored the advantages of quantifying our feelings using the Anxiety Scale, where we could track and compare our anxious feelings on different occasions and use this to reassure ourselves that no anxious feeling is permanent. The Anxiety Scale also helps us to identify and describe highly anxious moments in our life, such as episodes of frequent panic illustrated by the Loop of Peaking Anxiety.

Step Three

Part 3 of the book focuses on *understanding* the anxious mind. We discussed observing the dialogue that's ongoing between the 'rational' mind and the 'anxious' mind. Furthermore, I invited you to observe how your behaviour is affected by the Three Core Statements of Anxiety.

Part 3 also helped us to predict how the anxious mind can work, with emphasis on the Three Stages of 'Fight or Flight', as well as categorizing the intensity of our day-to-day behaviour using the Gear Analogy. This is the part of the book where we start to shift what we know about our anxiety into a more practical outlook.

Step Four

Part 4 looks at Training the Rational Mind. One of the most important factors in overcoming anxiety is the moderation of our negative *core beliefs*. Ultimately, if we don't believe that we're OK, then how can we convince the anxious mind otherwise? Part 4 looked at how behaviour can be powerful when it comes to habits and associations, and how neuropathways play a part in all of this.

We also looked at the concept of *self-reassurance* and how this is integral to nurturing a strong, positive core belief that we can cope if we find ourselves feeling anxious. Self-reassurance is best practised when we focus on changing our internal dialogue and promoting our own inner *nurturing parent* mode. We also looked at how the other modes of personality, according to the Transactional Analysis model, can play a part in living with anxiety.

Finally, Part 4 starts to explain the importance of present thinking with reference to how much our thoughts can be caught up in past and future thinking. The Thought Pie Chart was used to visualize this. We then started to discuss the non-coincidental nature of how we are at our calmest when our thoughts are predominantly in the present – leading us nicely into the final part of the book.

Step Five

Part 5 looks at our lifestyle choices and discusses the merits of popular practices such as exercise and meditation. While a healthy lifestyle is always to be encouraged, we looked at altering our expectations of the outcome of these activities with reference to the *'If I ...' plant* in Part 2.

Emphasis was placed on meditation as it promotes present thinking – something that our brain associates with not being anxious and which helps to stimulate the parasympathetic nervous system. Furthermore, meditation helps us to develop the skill of *observing* our thoughts. The better we are at observing our thoughts – particularly the negative ones – the more prepared we are to step aside from a thought and choose whether or not to engage with it emotionally. Meditation also helps us to observe our own *self-dialogue*; the way we speak to ourselves can play a crucial role in the generation of stress, but also in reassuring ourselves when we are anxious.

Part 5 also briefly outlines some of the different types of talking therapy available, before signing off with a reiteration of arguably the strongest message from my first book, *Anxiety: Panicking about Panic*, which is to go with your 'non-anxious you'.

The Panic Room®

The Panic Room is my personal counselling and coaching practice based in Manchester, England. From here, I work with individuals and run group workshops for people living with anxiety disorders. You can find out more by visiting:

www.thepanicroom.co.uk

The website includes useful information about anxiety, as well as information on events and recommended articles. I also have a Facebook page that you can follow, if you so desire.